TOURISM OPERATIONS

MTM-13

Notes For

Master of Tourism Management [MTM]

Useful For

IGNOU, KSOU (Karnataka), Bihar University (Muzaffarpur), Nalanda University, Jamia Millia Islamia, Vardhman Mahaveer Open University (Kota), Uttarakhand Open University, Kurukshetra University, Seva Sadan's College of Education (Maharashtra), Lalit Narayan Mithila University, Andhra University, Pt. Sunderlal Sharma (Open) University (Bilaspur), Annamalai University, Bangalore University, Bharathiar University, Bharathidasan University, HP University, Centre for distance and open learning, Kakatiya University (Andhra Pradesh), KOU (Rajasthan), MPBOU (MP), MDU (Haryana), Punjab University, Tamilnadu Open University, Sri Padmavati Mahila Visvavidyalayam (Andhra Pradesh), Sri Venkateswara University (Andhra Pradesh), UCSDE (Kerala), University of Jammu, YCMOU, Rajasthan University, UPRTOU, Kalyani University, Banaras Hindu University (BHU) and all other Indian Universities.

GullyBaba Publishing House Pvt. Ltd.

ISO 9001 & ISO 14001 CERTIFIED CO.

Regd. Office:
2525/193, 1st Floor, Onkar Nagar-A,
Tri Nagar, Delhi-110035
(From Kanhaiya Nagar Metro Station Towards Old Bus Stand)
Call: 9991112299, 9312235086
WhatsApp: 9350849407

Branch Office:
1A/2A, 20, Hari Sadan,
Ansari Road, Daryaganj,
New Delhi-110002
Ph.011-45794768
Call & WhatsApp:
8130521616,8130511234

E-mail: hello@gullybaba.com, **Website**: GullyBaba.com

New Edition

Author: Gullybaba.com Panel

Disclaimer

Although the author and publisher have made every effort to ensure that the information in this notes is correct, the author and publisher do not assume and hereby disclaim any liability to any party for any loss, damage, or disruption caused by errors or omissions, whether such errors or omissions result from negligence, accident, or any other cause.

If you find any kind of error, please let us know and get reward and or the new notes free of cost.

The notes is based on IGNOU syllabus. This is only a sample. The notes/author/publisher does not impose any guarantee or claim for full marks or to be passed in exam. You are advised only to understand the contents with the help of this notes and answer in your words.

All disputes with respect to this publication shall be subject to the jurisdiction of the Courts, Tribunals and Forums of New Delhi, India only.

About Publisher

Gullybaba Publishing House is the brainchild of Mr Dinesh Verma, his name alone evokes profound respect and admiration. He is the pioneer of providing quality materials to the students of IGNOU because, having been a student of IGNOU, he understood the difficulty and pain of the non-availability of quality materials himself. He is serving the students with the following services:

EXAM-SUCCESS GUIDES

Important questions, solved question papers, guess papers - all in one! to score good marks in lesser time and effort.

FREE BOOK

As our love and care for our students, here is a Free Gift – A Famous Book "Secrets to Pass IGNOU Exams with Less Study" for you. You can download it now! https://www.gullybaba.com/ignou-free/

YOUR CONTRIBUTION TO MOTHER-EARTH

When you read our books, you save our mother earth as we use recycled paper to make these books. On every purchase, we contribute something to plant a plant.

SOLVED ASSIGNMENTS PDFs / HAND-WRITTEN

Best and genuine solved assignments PDFs you can instantly download from Gullybaba.com or our App.

PROJECT REPORTS/SYNOPSIS

Best Quality No-Rejection projects/synopsis by professionals researchers in ready to refer format.

MOBILE APP

You can download 'Gullybaba' app from Google Play Store to enjoy all above services at one place.

Why Gullybaba's IGNOU Help Books

Is Fear of Exams making you stressful? Are you not getting good marks in your IGNOU exams? Are you looking for sure-shot solution get ahead in your IGNOU studies? Look no further than the answer: Gullybaba.com! With our expertly crafted course help-books, you'll be ready to face any exam with ease-guaranteed. What's more, we offer a huge discount on IGNOU Help Books Combo Deals – Save BIG.

Now, complete IGNOU courses more quickly and with Good Marks in Lesser Time & Effort.

Home Delivery of GPH Books

You can order Gullybaba Books online from Gullybaba.com or Gullybaba App. We dispatch books on the same day of receiving the order through our fastest courier partners.
You can also order books through WhatsApp on 9350849407 or by email at order@gullybaba.com.
We also provide "Cash On Delivery" through our courier partners and sometimes Govt. Postal Department.

Important Note to Sellers

Selling this book on any online platform like Amazon, Flipkart, Shopclues, Rediff, etc. without prior written permission of the publisher is prohibited and hence any sales by the SELLER will be termed as ILLEGAL SALE of GPH Books which will attract strict legal action against the offender.

Notable Information

An attempt has been carefully made to present this book more useful and meet the requirement and challenges of the course prescribed by IGNOU University. We hope that this effort will fulfil the readers' expectations and help them excel in exams. Referring to University study material alongside this book is like "icing on the cake".

We wish you a successful and rewarding career. If you have any feedback to improve our books/products, please email at feedback@gullybaba.com. Because we believe, "Feedback is breakfast of champions" and our readers are our strength.

Table of Contents

Question Papers

Chapter-1

UNDERSTANDING TOURISM OPERATIONS (Inter-Sectoral Linkages)

Q1. Discuss the inter-sectoral linkages in tourism operations. Give examples.

Ans. First of all we should know what inter-sectoral linkage is? The purchase and sale of goods and services between the various sectors of an economy – representing intermediate demand, refers to inter-sectoral linkages.

Tourism operations have created a space for themselves in the economy of each country, region or destination – small or big.

It is predictable insight that industry and commerce will boom at each end of any route, no matter, it seems where it starts or finishes. Evidences of this were seen in the boom tours of early railway bonanza. The same applies to holiday charter business. At the sunny end of developing charter routes – hotels, coach companies, bar-be-cues, beach bars, taxi firms and of course airports flourished and the supporting industry was quickly born. In those early days mystified and even frightened people looked at tour operators when they were explaining mysteries, dangers and wonders of far away places. At that time a seat on 250 miles per hour plane was a privilege. Without properly developed and efficiently utilised inter-sectoral linkages, these could not have become a commodity, as it is seen in the present scenario.

It is probably the advent of all-inclusive tour which necessitated the existence of linkages among different components of this sector. Essentially an all inclusive tour is a package of transport and accommodation and some other services which are sold as a single holiday for a single all inclusive price. This price is usually significantly lower than could be obtained by conventional methods of booking transport and accommodation separately from hotels and other suppliers.

Traditionally, only one destination was involved and normally an inclusive tour would not embrace the idea of touring different places. However, things have been changing as per the tastes and requirements of the consumers, i.e., the tourists. Today not just special but very-very special tours are packaged for different market segments under various types of tourism brands – from traditional cultural tourism to the most recent medicinal tourism. Then there are sub-types within these. For example, health tourism may have ayurvedic tourism with stay at an ayurvedic centre or surgery for an ailment plus leisure. The linkages, thus, go on expanding and the inter-dependence increases. This also makes quality management more difficult.

Even if you look at all the components which make up a conventional package tour and ask yourself to what degree, outside of choice, does a tour operator control the standards or quality that makes up a package holiday, you would find that following factors in the line of conventional package tour designing are beyond your control:

- Time spent at airports and services clients receive there,
- Time spent on an aeroplane; and the operating standards and services,
- The transfer to the hotel and back to airport,
- Services at the hotel itself,
- The surrounding environment, bars, cafes, etc.,
- The weather, and
- Local conditions.

One could, of course, argue the finer points of tour operator's role in these services and naturally a wise tour operator will have some control on their quality. This difference or USP is largely due to the kind of linkages you are able to establish with other components. Today survival is no less competitive but those who are in "winning positions" know how to harness their resources innovatively against the bottom line. It is no doubt true that only such people have turned Miami into a summer as well as a winter resort destination attracting millions of visitors all through the year.

Innovation, value addition, product differentiation and positioning, branding, pricing, etc., i.e., the various essentials for today's marketing have further expanded the line of linkages in tourism. These linkages are no more limited to packaging but are necessary for product growth as well as selling, etc.

Q2. Discuss the elements in tourism operations.

Ans. Different sections of each economy work in a closely-knit fashion. Tourism operations, however, are not an exception. The different key essentials in tour operations and the linkages involved therein, to a large extent, are common to all tourism businesses. However, there are problems that need attention. For example, initially, airlines were not ready to become a part of inter-sectoral linkage structure but when they realised that tour operators could fill the empty seats, they started offering special fares for use, exclusively by tour operators, for combining them into all-inclusive tours. But here also situations vary from country to country and destination to destination. These fares may be offered on some selected sectors only. We have seen that as a result of globalisation when certain countries opened their economies the number of business travellers increased manifold. The hotels jacked up the prices and airlines withdrew discounts or certain other incentives that were offered to tour operators. The sufferer was tourism and the tourist. Tensions emerged within the tourism industry sectors with each crying foul for the other. Charges and counter charges were made by one sector against the other with each sector's association taking up its cause. This, in fact, was an example to illustrate that the linkages are not necessarily always smooth and many a times you have to depend upon the collective strength of the association to determine the nature of linkages.

To base future growth purely on the availability of willing bodies should not be the sole strategy in this business. For example, in search for a special quality – USP – of a product the tour operators sought exclusive properties, quality airlines, etc. but they later on realised that they have no patent on these facilities or standards and they aren't difficult to emulate. Through such practices, they can only be a short term advantage that can be gained. Therefore, they had not only to satisfy the changing demand of tourists but also to coordinate the outside variables which make up an attractive package. It was acknowledged that they are operating and trying to dominate an industry where most of the ingredients that go to make up the product are outside their control. These factors may include:

- Price,
- Volume,
- Brands,
- Airline service,
- Uncontrollable costs, and
- Computerisation and use of technology, etc.

Let us discuss briefly some such factors in relation to tour operators' business as a case study though they are applicable in other tourism businesses also.

(1) Price: This is the most obvious area which concerns a tourist. Cutting the prices is easiest of all different marketing tasks. Reducing the price of a holiday can be done with a strike of pen but its advantages would only be short term. Your strategy should be to control the cost and to deliver the holiday sale at a profit. This calls for a well directed and well targeted strategy while focussing upon the following areas:

(i) Volume of customers (tourists),
(ii) Frequency of purchases (by tourists),
(iii) Distribution channels of your product,
(iv) Foreign currency regulations, and

(v) Overhead controls and product/service analysis.

In a highly competitive business like tourism pricing decisions are not easy. And further operating price decisions are even harder to take. For example, while pricing your package the approach of price-cutting should not only outrightly be adopted but it should be given a more creative approach. Since value is the key consumer watchword defined not just by price but also by product image, both above and below the line, it is the expression and presentation of values that counts. This is why holidays need to be packaged to offer high-perceived value even if in fact the basic package has not been altered. This, in fact, is done through some value additions. The tourists perceive the price cuts with a different perspective, i.e., the cut price is the actual price and the so called original price was profit inflated.

(2) Volume: Any knowledgeable tour operator will apprehend the fact that there are certain fixed/base costs which are not volume related, like the Managing Director's salary; computer technicians, office rentals, etc. These costs, however, are required to be spread over a large number of customers if your cost input is to remain competitive. For example, any tour operator carrying less than one million passengers will certainly have a higher per passenger cost than the consumer is prepared to pay unless the services/products are really unique and special. As a strategic tour operator you should know that higher volume of business can be achieved through large scale advertising and publicity for your company. It not only gives better ability to your customers to buy at competitive prices but it will also allow your advertising cost to be more meaningful. Not only this, it also establishes national brand awareness with profound effects on the willingness of retailer to display your product at their shelves. Therefore, volume shall be seen as a vital ingredient and factor in deciding the per-passenger cost input which could only be delivered and achieved by a well-directed strategy.

(3) Brands: Just to recapitulate, we can say that multi-branding, mainly serves two purposes:

- achieves more speedily the proper economic volume levels, and
- services the changing requirements of tourists more readily.

As a small tour operator you can create your own identity. For example, "Operator X", a small tour operator who specialises in Greek islands, could sell readily this special package. However, from the tour operation brochures produced for mass tourism he could not get much business. In comparison to him a large tour operator may not perform well for Greek islands market but may do well in mass tourism market. It clearly means that "X" has earned brand equity for the niche market. Therefore, you shall not allow your need for volume of business for the sake of economics to deny yourself access to these potentially important and yet more individual markets.

(4) Airline seats: The one important component of your product, which in every sense of the world is a commodity, is the seat on an aircraft. Of course, there are preferred carriers; and yes, it is worth for airline to maintain high standards and reputation, but it is also true that only a small percentage of passengers carried by these airlines even would know the name and type of aircraft they are booked on to travel. The cost of aircraft seats and, therefore, the profit of an airline will largely depend upon the relationship between the airline and the tour operators. At present 90-95% of leisure holidaymakers book themselves on airlines or accommodation through tour operators operating in their area of residence or work. But how long this will continue remains a question as the use of internet is fast affecting the marketing and distribution channels.

(5) Uncontrollable costs: Tourism industry is probably the only industry which has bent under so many pressures, like pressure of consumer bargaining; frequent fluctuation in currency value; that it shall prejudge the cost of fuel and prejudge the whim of government to increase local taxes and levy increased landing charges, etc. To overcome this, the principal service providers, be it an airline or a hotelier, give no guarantee for surcharges. A tour operator sets the prices of his products fourteen or more months before the arrival of his clients at destination. Therefore, when the principal supplier gives no guarantee on surcharges and tour operator has to sell his package so much in advance, linkages are bound to be stronger so as to avoid any confrontation related to price, quality or standard of services.

(6) Linkages with technology providers: If a person wants to travel by air he/she will need a ticket; which provides him/her right of passage and in return the airline needs to reserve a seat in his/her name. The person also needs to book himself/herself for a hotel room at the destination and hence, the hotel ought to really expect him/her. It is very difficult to imagine these economic transactions in a better-suited business environment related to the wonders of modern technology. To solve many travel and reservation related problems tour operators must develop and maintain linkages with manufacturer/suppliers of computers and designers of software required by them. Development and regular updating of Amadeus and Galelio are remarkable examples of these linkages.

(7) Quality management operations: In the present globalised competitive business environment quality management is the key word for success in any business and tour operation is not an exception. You may be representing any sector of travel trade in your operation if this element of quality control or quality assurance is missing you cannot sustain in the market. Quality management is advised to begin with product design and shall remain as a continuous process all through the stages of product development up to post consumption stage. For instance, if you are a manufacturer or supplier of airline seats it is important for you to control the quality of your product not only in terms of its comfort, location, and convenience but also in terms of its sale, and related facilities and services like emergency landing facilities to combat terrorist or hijack situation, so on and so forth.

In your operations you shall ensure a high degree quality while preparing and presenting your products or services; failing which the result is dissatisfaction of passengers. This dissatisfaction will lead to multiplication of lost passengers through word of mouth bad publicity. Therefore, significance of quality management cannot and shall not be ignored in tour operation business.

(8) Value addition in operations: Gone are the days of monopolistic market conditions. Today, customer is well aware of the existence of alternative products and alternative suppliers. Therefore, to be a successful tour operator or manager in tourism business you must lay emphasis upon value addition to your operation. For instance, if you are a tourist transport operator and if you provide cold drinks to your passengers after every stopover for sightseeing or if you are a hotelier and you provide free transport for transfers of your groups, or if you are an airline operator you decide to add some recreational activities, e.g., fashion show, magic shows, etc., on board all this will add to the satisfaction level of your customers. All such value added activities offered by you will provide you with repeat as well as referred business.

Hence, value added services can be integrated both horizontally and vertically within other sectors of the tourism trade.

(9) Trained service providers: Tourism and hospitality being important components of travel trade are characterised by a common characteristic, i.e., man served by another man. This characteristic has overemphasised the significance of trained service providers. For instance, if you are a provider of tourist transport services, it is essential for you to provide a trained driver, assistant as well as a trained escort with the group. It is true that this trade is so diversified as are the training needs, but as a professional operator you shall assess the needs for training and must train your workforce accordingly to provide best services to your customer. If you practice this advice nothing can prevent you from becoming a successful entrepreneur in tourism trade.

Q3. What do you understand by the term 'Operations management'.

Ans. Operations management focuses on carefully managing the processes to produce and distribute products and services. Usually, small businesses don't talk about "operations management", but they carry out the activities that management schools typically associate with the phrase "operations management." Major, overall activities often include product creation, development, production and distribution.

Measures: A service organisation addresses the requirements of its customers using a service delivery system and provides the required services. Service organisations respond to the requirements of customers to satisfy their needs through a service delivery process and leave certain impressions in the minds of their customers. Typical examples include management consultancies, automobile garages, hotels, hospitals and banks. A service organisation may not always make use of material input and may not always produce products that are used by customer. For instance, a law firm providing legal consultancy to its clients may not provide material inputs to the system or produce material output, the input and output are informational and experiential in nature. On the other hand, in the case of other service systems, such as an automobile garage, a restaurant and a health care system, there are material inputs and material outputs (in the form of products consumed by the customers, as in the case of a restaurant). Despite this difference, service systems also have a conversion process that utilize resources and delivers useful output from the system.

An operations system is defined as one in which several activities are performed to 'transform' a set of inputs into a useful output using a transformation process. These inputs and outputs can be physical things such as materials and/or informational and experiential things. Viewed in this manner, we can say that manufacturing and service systems could be broadly classified as operations systems. Operations management is a systematic approach to address all the issues pertaining to the transformation process that converts some inputs outputs that are useful, and could fetch revenue for the organisation. Four aspects of this definition merit closer attention:

(1) A systematic approach involves understanding the nature of issues and problems to be studied, establishing measures of performance, collecting relevant data, using scientific tools and techniques and solution methodologies to analyse and developing effective as well as efficient solution to the problem at hand. Therefore, for successful operations management, the focus should be on developing a set of tools and techniques to analyse problems faced within an operations system.

(2) The second aspect of operations management pertains to addressing several issues that an organisation faces. These issues vary markedly in terms of the time horizon, the nature of the problem to be solved and the commitment of the required resources, simple problems include deciding how to re-route jobs when a machine breaks down on a shop floor or how to handle a surge in demand in a service system. On the other hand, decisions such as where to locate the plant, what capacity to build in the system and what types of products and services need to be offered to the customers, require greater commitment of resources and time. Operations

management provides alternative methodologies to address such wide-ranging issues in an organisation.

(3) Transformation processes are central to operations systems. The transformation process ensures that inputs are converted into useful output. Therefore, the focus of the operations management discipline is to address the various aspects of design in the transformation process as well as planning and operational control.

(4) Finally, in the goal of operations management is to ensure that through careful planning and control of the operations the organisation is able to keep costs to the minimum and obtain revenue in excess of costs. In order to ensure this, an appropriate performance evaluation system is required. Therefore, the operations management discipline also involves the development of such a system of performance evaluation and methods by which the operating system could make improvements to meet marked presentation trial.

Chapter-2

RESPECTING RESIDENT CONCERNS IN TOURISM OPERATIONS AND DEVELOPMENT

Q1. Discuss the relevance of concern of residents in tourism operations.

Ans. If you want to encourage tourism in your area/community you will have to focus on the concerns of the residents. This is necessary because the local residents should neither feel neglected nor remain dissatisfied with their share in the development of tourism. It is always desired by the local residents that benefits derived from tourism should come to them.

An important aspect of planning that has been emphasised for some time is community involvement in planning process and decision making. This is based on the concept that planning is for the residents of an area. They should be given the opportunity to participate in the planning of its future development and express their views on the type of future environment they want to live in.

Community involvement requires more time to be allocated to the planning process and a debate on issues concerning the residents. Implications of various types of development features or scenarios are available to the community. Under normal circumstances, in most of the developing countries, we plan for development of infrastructure and superstructure but we pay little or no attention on concerns of residents at planning level. There is ample research to prove that if residents concerns were ignored hostilities emerged at the destinations and the negative impacts of tourism were visible all over. For tourism operations at the local level, one must plan for the following areas of concern:

(1) Health and Security Concerns: This is an important area which calls for special concern of the residents. If we look at vaccination routines being followed in our country as a normal procedure it clearly indicates at health hazards which comes with tourists, whether they are domestic or international. Today AIDS carriers are not only from other lands, but also from within our country. Surveys reveal that tourists coming from certain regions have a tendency to test positive for AIDS or other communicable diseases. While planning tourism operations you should place this residents' concern at the forefront. If precautions are not taken in this direction, consequences can be irreparable.

When a large number of tourists visit a place it is naturally exposed to security threats. When strangers come to your town, their background, intentions and plans are not known to you. Various acts of terrorism have proved this point beyond doubt. You must keep in view the security concerns of local residents. As a planner for tourism operations you must consider these concerns because losses as a result of lapses on either of these fronts would lead to disasters and destinations will earn a bad image. Once this happens, a lot of investment in terms of money and efforts will be required for its improvement.

(2) Vehicle Parking Concern: With any destination reaching stages of mass tourism, one of the immediate problems it faces is that of parking tourist vehicles. With increasing number of vehicles in urban cities, even residents find it difficult to have parking for their own vehicles.

You cannot expect problem-free parking for your visitors. Hence, you should prioritise this concern of visitors whenever you are planning for tourism development. For example, in New Delhi, if you visit any one of the most frequented monuments, be it Red Fort, Qutab Minar, or Bahai Temple, you are bound to face parking problem. Not only this when these visitors go to district shopping centres they use parking space meant for or designed for local residents. This clearly opens the doors for hostility between hosts and visitors. However, if you have planned in such a manner that the parking concern has been taken account of then your destination would score a point. For example, today if you go to Shimla or Mussoorie or Nainital, the most crowded destinations by visitors, parking is a problem for both residents and visitors. On the other hand, when you go to Disney World which has a land area of approximately 9 acres, the built up area is only 2.5 acres, and remaining area is left open for parking of tourist vehicles. This means residents concern has been taken into account while planning it. Hence, We should also plan our attractions on the patterns of such established models which have shown examples of tremendous parking management. In fact, vehicle parking is very much an operational concern also. Congested parking areas can cause delays in tour operations.

(3) Transportation Concern: Transportation consideration is particularly important because it provides access to the places of tourist interest. You can classify local transportation system into three levels:

(i) Trunk or main roads linking the provincial and larger urban centres to one another and the capital of state;

(ii) Provincial roads distributing traffic from the provincial centres to district centres of each province; and

(iii) Local roads providing a network of tracks connecting places of interest with provincial and district centres.

As a result of tourism development in any area residents concerns are more oriented towards level 2 and level 3. At this point local residents find that transportation resources available and meant for them are also used by foreign and domestic tourists. This makes the availability of transport for local people difficult. In return this creates unrest among them and finally tourists face the humiliation. To overcome this situation, transportation facilities and services should be planned and managed while giving leverage for a particular number of domestic and international tourists in your destination area. Moreover, length and width of roads connecting various points of interest for visitors, like, monuments, district centres, art galleries, museums, cinema theatres, etc. shall be planned carefully so that traffic movements remain smooth and do not cause

inconvenience to the local residents. Therefore, residents shouldn't feel that due to increasing number of visitors' traffic jams have started taking place. On the other hand, visitors shouldn't feel disappointed due to traffic jams on every road in the place of their visit.

(4) Infrastructural Concerns: The terms "infrastructure" planning refers to those forms of construction on or below the ground that provides the basic framework for effective functioning of development system such as tourism industry and urban areas. Adequate infrastructure is essential for the successful development of tourism in developing countries like India, which have serious infrastructural constraints. These areas may include transportation facilities and services, sewage disposal, drainage, electric power and telecommunication services, etc. If you look at this list you will agree that these services cannot be planned particularly for tourists.

While planning them for local residents concerns of tourists/visitors must also be taken into account and while developing infrastructural facilities for tourists interests of local residents must be kept in view. For instance, when Neemrana Fort Palace was being developed by private developers after taking it on lease from Rajasthan Government, basic infrastructural amenities were missing. They developed not only roads, electric power, sewage and disposal system, water lines, telephone lines, gasolines but they also built schools and hospitals for local residents. This clearly indicates at the basic infrastructure of an area that serves general community and economic development needs can often serve tourism with only moderate expansion. In turn, infrastructure built or improved to serve tourism can serve general community needs. In fact, this multiple use of infrastructure with tourism helping to pay for infrastructure costs can be one of the socio-economic benefits of tourism. However, in some cases, such as, an isolated resort at Muketeswar, where there is no infrastructure, you will have to develop all required infrastructural amenities for tourists only.

(5) Super-Structural Concerns: In small destinations superstructure is designed for the usage of local residents and when large number of visitors visit them, these super-structural facilities get overcrowded. For instance, a bus or rail terminal is used by both local residents and visitors. As a result, there terminals are crowded and many undesired and unwanted experiences are experienced by all.

All these add to dissatisfaction of both the tourists and local residents have to bear extra cost of commodities which otherwise is affordable only to visitors. The line of contention here is that as a result of visits of affluent tourists to these small destinations cost of commodities go up which is largely due to the fact that vendors have to maintain décor, cleanliness and hygenity in and around their shopping centres to attract foreign tourists. Moreover, they have to pay commission to brokers, who lure the tourists to their shops from t hese district centres. Therefore, you should keep in view concern of residents from this perspective that shopping centres of local residents should be avoided for shopping by visitors and for this special shopping complexes must be planned and developed for tourists, e.g., Palika Bazar, Ansal Plaza, Sahara Mall, etc. Besides price rise, at many destinations, tourism also creates scarcities. Water shortage, electricity shortage and power cuts, shortages of essential commodities, etc. are attributed to tourist influx.

You are already familiar with the concept of carrying capacity and applying it in your operations can be a good solution. Not only this, even accommodation units shall be built out of residential colonies so as to escape from the chances of price speculation of land as well as inflation of prices of other related commodities in these residential colonies. Ancillary products of these accommodation units like restaurants, coffee homes, nightclubs, bars, discotheques, etc. should be developed keeping in view interests of local residents. If you keep entry fees for discotheques or swimming pool or health clubs of these accommodation units too high, local residents may feel alienated. In other

words, they will get the feeling that on their own land th ey are deprived from entry in these ancillary stations of the hotels.

It is at both levels, i.e., when you plan super -structural facilities or when you use them in your operations you should keep in view the feelings of local residents. This can be done by allowing them to participate not only in policy decisions but also by giving them proper training and education and if possible employment. This will help in creating a healthy environment and better relationship between the tourism industry and the residents or the host population.

(6) Environmental Concerns: Tourism relies heavily upon the use of environment to a large extent in the area of development under consideration. If environment is exploited without caring for or giving proper leverage to the residents' concern, tourism operations are bound to be adversely affected. More particularly today, when people have become so much conscious about their health, they desire to have a green belt extending over large areas. Therefore, while planning any activity, you should carefully analyse the fact that to what extent it would disturb the ecoenvironment of that area. If it is at minimum level, you shall proceed but if it is of quite high level then consequences should be borne in mind while proceeding with such developments and consensus of local residents should be received before executing such plans.

Today hotels, the element which was believed to be the most polluting component of tourism has become eco-conscious (eco-tels) and they are adopting all precautionary measures to sustain the environment of the area where they are operating. The same kind of approach shall be adopted by other components of tourism industry. Hence, as a tour operator or travel agent you shall advise your clients and groups on environment-friendly programmes of local residents of the areas they are visiting so that when they arrive in these cities they are well versed with rules and regulation of environment friendly society. For instance, when you plan a visit to Singapore you are told by your agent/operator about cleanliness, hygenity and low degree of noise pollution being practised in Singapore. For example, if you are noticed throwing waste or shouting loudly on the roads fines are imposed. Air pollution is another aspect which the tourist transport operators should take care off.

(7) Socio-Cultural Concerns: Modern tourists may not visit a destination for a single attraction, but he/she visits a mixed blend of attractions at the destination. Various types of cultural festivals related to local tradition and arts are one of the major attractions. Large religious festivals and pageants such as carnival in Rio de Janeiro, Mardi Grasin, New Orleans and Pera Hera in Kandy, Winter Festival at Beijing, Puri festival, Elephant Boat Race at Kerala and many more festivals of same kind which attract not only the foreign tourists but also the local residents. It, therefore, becomes important that concerns of local residents must be taken in to account while planning or organising such events whatever may be the size of activity.

It has been noticed globally that in large number of cases where tourism development has occurred along with it social unrest or friction has also emerged. For instance, in Fiji, Spain, Romania and at many more places , destinations and attractions have been developed keeping in view the interests, liking, dislikings and tastes of visitors and not that of local residents. As a result local residents have felt alienated with such development. For example, in Romania, nightclubs were developed only for foreigners and local residents were not allowed. The very first reaction of local residents was that all these attractions and activities have been developed at their costs or from the money that they have paid as taxes to federal governments. Therefore, it was argued that they couldn't be deprived of facilities which are built using the resources meant for them. This created social unrest among local residents and for some time this was an unpopular destination among foreign tourists.

Another significant activity which is catching up with both domestic and international tourists is gambling casinos. In developed countries, this doesn't carry much of the social difference but in case of developing country like India which is characterised as a conservative society wherein gambling is still a privilege of only 2-5% of society, it is still taken to be as social evil. Thus, while developing such a product you must respect residents concerns or else your product may have to face lot of social and political disagreement.

Physical Land Use Concern is equally important because whatever facilities or services you plan in a destination they should be in line with the blue print or master plan of development for the region. In many cases it has been observed that when attempts were made by planners or developers to convert areas earmarked for public utilities or services like hospitals, schools, religious places, open parks and spaces for children, etc. into commercial establishments, like shopping cum office complexes or commercial recreational centre, objections were raised by Residents Association.

However, even after this if you developed the desired facility for visitors; local residents shall always remain hostile to such developments. When tourists start coming to this area and they intend to mix up with local residents of the area, their cold reaction makes tourists uncomfortable. Though they utilise these services but the kind of interaction they expect wouldn't come up. Hence, it is advisable that you must plan physical land use of the area in such a manner that developmental activities take place in consent with that of local residents and experiences of tourists and visitors to that area would be pleasant and memorable.

Another important consideration while planning of physical land use of tourism development is to keep in view the personal privacy of residents. If you are planning a multi-storey shopping complex in front of a residential colony, you must keep in mind that it will naturally encroach upon the privacy of these residents. Moreover, the kind of nuisance this commercial development may generate also demands your consideration. The local residents will and are always concerned with postdevelopment results both in terms of advantages it will render as well as the disadvantages it will bring to them.

Regular interaction with residents as a tourism professional can bear good results for your venture. Such regular interaction provides a common platform to both, the residents and developers of tourist facilities. Using this platform, the residents can raise their concerns and interests so as to enable developers or operators to organise their activities in such a manner so that both the parties are mutually benefited. Moreover, if activities are designed and executed in line with mutual coordination, probabilities of unrest or dissatisfaction are minimised. Consequently, it is desirable that residents' concerns must be bear in mind at both pre-planning and post-planning stages.

Q2. Discuss the relationship between host resident concerns and tourism development.

Ans. Without a doubt the unbelievable growth of intercontinental tourism has brought about hasty changes in terms of economic growth. Narrowing down the cultural gap and fostering universal brotherhood are the other projected benefits of tourism. However, World Tourism Organis ation (WTO) has summarised highlights of tourism growth in 2000 as:

"Tourism clearly counts as one of the most remarkable economic and social phenomena of the last century. It undoubtedly will keep this position for the century to come. Every year a bigger portion of the world population takes part in tourism activity and for the majority of countries tourism has developed as one of the most dynamic and fastest sector of the economy."

The world has seen tourism as a challenge to enhance opportunities for both tourists and residents. Since 1950s the international tourist arrivals have increased by twenty times, i.e., number has gone up from 25 million in 1950 to 639 million in 2002. WTO's forecast predicts that this number would go up to 977 million tourists by 2010. It wouldn't be an exaggeration to say that across the world tourism ranks among top five foreign exchange earner in 83 countries whereas in not less than 38 countries tourism forms the backbone of their economies. As a result of these changes 8% of total export earnings of goods and services worldwide are contributed by tourism. Various factors which have facilitated this growth are increased availability of leisure due to specialisation of labour, lifestyle and work related changes, like flexi time, working from home, sharing of employment, last but not the least technological changes. It is very well said that travel and tourism will be as good as technology allows it to be. The benefits which tourism development strives for the local residents ar e manifold. It not only improves economic condition of the local residents but also on socio-cultural front, the benefits for local residents are apparent. For instance, when tourism grows in an area, both the life partners get an opportunity to work in any of the trades related to tourism. This obviously enhances their purchasing power and thereby providing exposure to them which hitherto wouldn't have been possible. As a result of socio-economic development in the locality manifold changes and benefits come to the local residents. These benefits can also be seen in the form of regional development. The best strategy would be to avoid the harmful impacts and encourage helpful ones through your operations.

Q3. It is not appropriate to use the same set of principles for managing the operations in manufacturing and service organization. Comment over this statement.

Ans. Operations traditionally refers to the production of goods and services separately, although the distinction between these two main types of operations is increasingly difficult to make as manufacturers tend to merge product and service offerings. More generally, Operations Management aims to increase the content of value-added activities in any given process. Fundamentally, these value-adding creative activities should be aligned with market opportunity for optimal enterprise performance.

Generally services are classified separately from manufacturing in a macroeconomic sense, from the perspective of operations management, the separation is artificial. From the operations management perspective the notion of a 'pure product' and 'pure service' is just two ends of the spectrum. In reality, a vast majority of operations share a continuum of services and products. Therefore, most of the principles and tools and techniques of operations management apply to both these sectors.

Services such as management consulting, health spas and education have dominant service attributes. They form one end of the spectrum. Similarly, manufacture and supply of machine tools, gadgets and consumables have a dominant product attribute and they form the other end of the spectrum. However, several others share both service and product attribute. In the case of a restaurant, the food items share both the products and services attributes. A closer examination of the figure illustrates the important differences between services and manufacturing.

Table : GDP growth of service sectors in India

	1998-99	1999-00	2000-01	2001-02	2002-03	2003-04
	Service Sector Growth rates in GDP (% change over last year					
Service (Overall)	8.4	10.1	5.5	6.8	7.9	9.1
Trade, Hotels, Transport, Communications	7.7	8.5	6.8	9.0	9.8	11.8
Financial Services	7.4	10.6	3.5	4.5	8.7	7.1
Community, Social & Personal Services	10.4	12.2	5.2	5.1	3.9	5.8

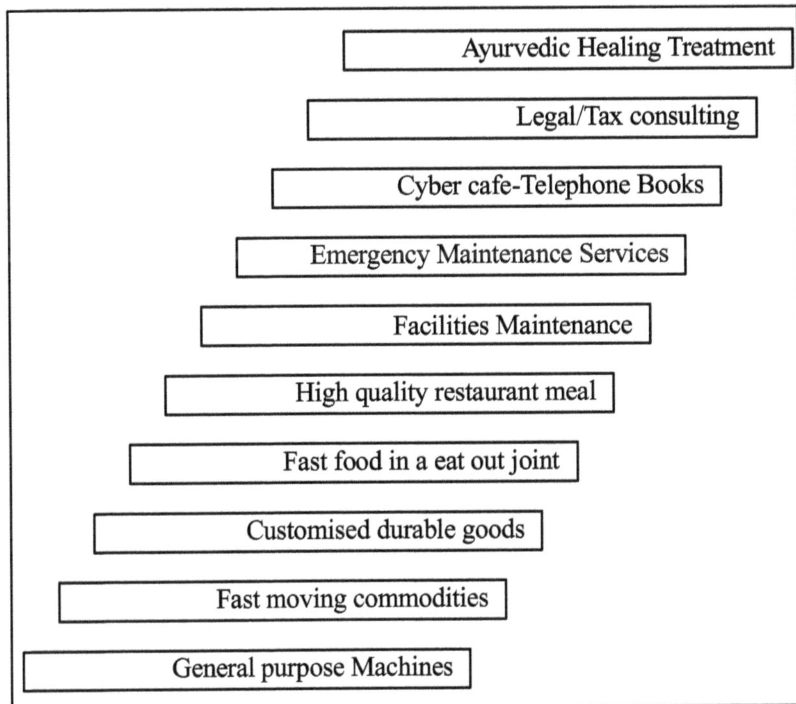

Intangibility: Fundamentally, services differ from manufacturing with respect to tangibility. Because services are performances and actions rather than objects, they cannot be touched, tasted or felt as in the case of objects. There is nothing to touch or feel in the case of a consulting assignment or education. At the most, the recipients of services can form an opinion (based on some personal assessment) about the quality of the service offered. This has important implications for defining and assessing the service quality. In contrast, in a product oriented operation, the product is defined by certain attributes and the customer faces less ambiguity with respect to the product, its attributes and performance. The customer can touch and feel and make his/her own assessment of the product.

Heterogeneity: The second differentiating aspect of services is the high degree of heterogeneity. Since the experiential component is dominant in a service, it is likely that no two services are exactly alike. The differences are attributed to the differences in the service receives (customers), the services providers and other parameters of the service delivery system. Therefore, a dentist attending to two consecutive patients having identical aliments may provide more or less the same type of service. Nevertheless, the two patients may have different perceptions of the quality of the service and may have different satisfaction levels. Moreover, the time spent by the dentist in both the cases could be highly variable. High heterogeneity means high variability in the operations system performance and the need to factor them into planning and control of the operations.

Simultaneous Production and Consumption: More often, service happens in the presence of the customer and the customer may also be involved at the time the service is produced for his/her consumption. In the previous example, the doctors and the patients are in the together to produce and consume the service. Similar is the case of education, entertainment, travel, tourism and hotel services. On the other hand, in the case of manufacturing, most goods are produced at some point in time and distributed to the customer later. From a service operations point of view, what this implies is that the degree of customers contact is likely to be high and this need to be taken into consideration white a service delivery system is designed planned and controlled for operations. Of late, the use of technology has helped organisation shift some of the traditional operations from a predominantly service domain to the product domain. One such example is the installation of ATMs for money withdrawal. In this case, by the use of technology, the degree of customer contact is significantly reduced and simultaneous production and consumption of the service eliminated.

Perishability: Services also have the characteristic of perishability. By this we mean services cannot be inventoried. Thirty minutes of a doctor's consulting expertise today cannot be stored for future use or reused or returned in a future period. Similarly, the treatment for acute headache likely to be faced by a patient sometime in the future cannot be stored in advance and reused at that time. Such possibilities of inventorying the supply and demand occurring at one point in time and using it at a later time are very common in a manufacturing system. The implication for operations is that service systems require methods that work without inventories.

The above characteristics of services apply to a 'pure service', which is move experiential in nature. Furthermore, businesses with dominant service characteristics will have these features dominating over the other product related features. For examples, in the case of a fast food joint, there is both the service aspect and the product aspect. A customer having one plate of idli with sambar experiences all the above attributes when viewed from the service angle. However, there is also a product angle to the restaurant. For instance, viewing idli as a product may enable the restaurant owner to inventory them for future use.

Chapter-3

QUALITY MANAGEMENT AND CUSTOMER CARE

Q1. Write an essay on quality control and customer care.

Ans. Quality control is a process by which entities review the quality of all factors involved in production. This approach places an emphasis on three aspects:

- Elements such as controls, job management, defined and well managed processes, performance and integrity criteria, and identification of records.
- Competence, such as knowledge, skills, experience, and qualifications.
- Soft elements, such as personnel integrity, confidence, organizational culture, motivation, team spirit, and quality relationships.

The basic goal of quality control is to ensure that the products, services, or processes provided meet specific requirements and are dependable, satisfactory, and fiscally sound.

Quality control: The use of the thought of Quality Management in tourism operations emerged when many countries realised that all tourists are not the same. They are dissimilar on the basis of their origin, travel purpose, length of stay, activities, etc. For instance Japanese, Germans and other North American tourists are often thought to be particularly great spenders. As a consequence to this many countries have developed their services to meet the needs of such a kind of segmented tourist market. Because of this many countries/destinations started announcing that they want quality tourists. However, the assumption here that a high spender will also be a quality consumer in relation to various sensitivities still remains a question mark . There can be a situation where a high spender because of his/her high purchasing power may become more exploitative of tourism resources. Some countries have discovered that the market (being highly segmented) is to be linked to the available resources and infrastructure at the destinations. This led to another kind of approach wherein it was not just the quality of products and services was to be taken into account but the quality of users of such products or services was also to be ensured. In other words, if one tourist spends as much as three others combined, the absolute impact and resource use of former is likely to be smaller and, therefore, cost benefit ratio would be more favourable.

It is, therefore, widely acknowledged that 1980s saw many service providers in North America responding to a perceived 'quality' crisis posed by products offered by rivals as a method of retaining the market share. Hence, if late 1980s was characterised by a business environment committed to quality early 1990s was dominated by the Total Quality Management, a more sophisticated form of recognising customer's needs as an integral part of an organisation's goals.

Quality management, from the perspective of making cost-benefit ratio depends upon several factors, such as, the time reference unit of expenditure, i.e., expenditure per day/expenditure per trip, how much money is spent on providing it as well as leakages involved in it, the sectoral and regional patterns of expenditure, and government's objectives and goals in this direction.

However, before you decide upon what constitutes quality in tourism services, you should clearly define your own objectives of service quality (Quality Policy) and your target market. In the absence of such a framework quantity in tourism may not be the quality in tourism. Certain tourism industry sectors as stated earlier, link the parameters of quality with the purchasing power of the tourists. To some extent this may be in line with most often mentioned objectives of tourism development, like, increase in foreign exchange earnings, improving the balance of payments, and increased income earned through tourism and allied industries. But economists believe that taking in account the per day expenditure of tourists may always not be a correct measure as these high daily expenditures go hand in hand with short length of stay. In many cases they argue that tourists with the highest per day expenditure are not those with highest per capita or per trip expenditure. Hence, merely focussing upon per day expenditure of tourist may not be in line with the overall earnings from tourism.

Moreover, in such cases tourism does not benefit everybody in the host community equally and some form of tourism may be more regionally or sectorally based than others since expenditures by tourists with a short length of stay are more likely to be concentrated in the primary tourist destinations and international gateways. Those tourists who turn out to be visitors with very low daily expenditure may in fact turn out to be quality tourists as far as the destination's concerns are to be accounted for. They may care for local resources, respect, local customs instead of exploiting them, and may live with them in harmony. Thus, they may turn out to be quality tourists from the point of view of the sustainability of the destination. Therefore, quality operations in tourism have to be linked not just with high spending but also to the guiding principles of tourism in that area and the satisfaction of both tourists as well as hosts.

The 1990's Quality Management is of great concern to tourism operations for both academicians and practitioners. This is largely due to increasing interest and concern for customer care and satisfaction.

Therefore, it can be seen as one all-embracing approach enabling an organisation to develop a more holistic view of customers, quality issues and service provisions as an ongoing process linked with the quality perception of the hosts. There is always a problem of establishing a universal definition of "quality" which could be applied to different sectors of tourism operations. Townsend and Gebhart (1986) distinguished between the subjective evaluation of quality by the customer (quality of perception) and providers more objective assessment (quality of fact). Clearly the meaning of quality will vary according to the context and perceptions of who is establishing what, and what can be deemed as quality. But this concept in tourism operations requires organisations to work towards specific goals focussed on an agreed concept of quality. Corporate commitment is required so that Quality Management permeates from all areas of company business. Quality management will also provide you with an opportunity to monitor and implement internal procedures and to control suppliers using established quality standards and procedures.

One of the real challenges for Quality Management in tourism operations is to establish or determine what customers consider as excellence in service provision and design of service delivery system so as to deal with individual tourist's requests, requirements and needs. Many players in the tourism industry have started targeting the individual customers by adding value to their products through an analysis of what the individual perceived as quality. Naturally, the costing and pricing both go up in such cases. Others in this sector have attempted to provide budget category of tourists. It is at the strategic policy and planning level that the tourism service provider may need to agree on how to improve continuously on the quality front in providing the services so that the tourists experience is enhanced. One challenge in this endeavour will be to ensure that the process of travel is not perceived as a mundane and stressful experience by tourists.

Whatever be the stage, implementing a Quality Management strategy is not an easy task for service providers where it may involve a change in corporate culture. Nevertheless, if management is willing seriously to embrace certain principles, then the management strategies will prove to be the key to successful implementation of Quality Management in tourism operations.

As a manager if you wish to implement successfully Quality management strategies you are advised to consider following points:

- You should have long term commitment to constant improvement,
- You should have a culture of "right first time",
- Your employees need to be trained to understand customer-supplier relationships,
- While purchasing you should not just focus upon price but take in to account the total cost and quality,
- You should manage improvements in delivery system,
- You should introduce new methods of super vision and training,
- In order to improve communication and build teamwork you should breakdown interdepartmental barriers. This will also help you in managing the service process well,
- You should develop Human Resource Strategies (on the job training, inc entives and motivation) so as to develop experts and specialists in your work force, and
- Last not the least you must develop systematic approach to manage the overall implementation of Quality Management programme in your organisation.

In nutshell we can say that the implementation of Quality Management Programme can be shaped by applying the above stated principles and their outcome can be experienced in following areas:

- improved Customer-service provider-relationships,
- better managing processes,
- change in organisational culture, and
- commitment of employees.

These outcomes, of course, are accompanied by necessities of a system based on national or international standards as well as tools to analyse and predict what type of corrective action is needed to improve quality or how to monitor progress of such corrective actions. A strong Management Information System backed by feed back from customers as well as front-line employees will also help you in quality management.

Customer care: Customer service is a series of activities designed to enhance the level of customer satisfaction – that is, the feeling that a product or service has met the customer expectation. In tourism business, the main task of the manager includes providing quality service to the tourists. This naturally includes the concept of customer care. If you ignore this you will find it difficult to attract

customers. Both in the field of inbound and outbound tour operations there is a fierce competition to win and retain clients. Only those who really provide good customer care have a hope and scope for surviving in the business of tourism.

Always remember that you are operating in the field of specialised services wherein your clients have high expectations of the services you provide or you can provide. Meeting these expectations by your company largely depends upon how good you are at your job as a manager. You can either make their dreams come true or turn their dreams in to nightmares. On the one hand you have a situation wherein when these expectations are not met the customers remain unhappy or on the other hand, you deliver your services with the quality beyond their expectations and hopes. Remember, that many of your clients might be experienced ones who would compare your services and product with their previous experiences. Customer satisfaction is achieved not only by giving them value for money but also by winning them for repeat business and good publicity. Best example of caring for your clients and ensuring that they enjoy a high quality service is that before delivering the service develop certain checks and test that you are ready or not. Besides, to offer a quality service to every client means being able to maintain high standards and to repeat them every time. It also involves developing new systems and making them work to attain your organizations' value and customer approval associated goals. You must always remember that each of your customer would like to feel special and making each one feel different from thousands of others is not always easy. However, a beginning can be made through effective use of communication skills or your front-line staff should be trained to:

- Always acknowledge the customer,
- Smile and mean it,
- Address people courteously,
- Look them in the eye when while speaking to them, and
- If known, use their name.

Q2. Discuss the concept of Quality management in service industry.

Ans. Quality management can be considered to have three main components: quality control, quality assurance and quality improvement. Quality management is focused not only on product/service quality, but also the means to achieve it. Quality management therefore uses quality assurance and control of processes as well as products to achieve more consistent quality.

The concept of quality as excellence has now been largely superseded by definitions emphasising upon quality issues related to production or delivery mechanisms. Also, a new dimension added to this is the perception of the quality by the consumers. Some present definitions confirm requirements for zero defects to relate quality with product and manufacturing specifications whereas others tackle quality from customers' perception and satisfaction level. We are also focusing upon the concept of quality management in this Unit as an important challenge being faced by tourism industry to reconcile the quality of services actually produced with that perceived by the tourists. This notion has given birth to a theoretical model, designed by Nightingale (1985), who identifies two qualities of the service offering as perceived by provider and that of the service received by the consumer. This has been successfully refined by Parashraman et al (1985) into 'gap model' identifying five discrepancies or 'gaps' which may develop in the service supply process and interface with the

service experiences as shown in Table below .

Sl.	Designation	Location
1	Positioning	Between management perception of customer expectation and expectation them selves.
2	Specifications	Between management perceptions of customer expectation and actual service specified.
3	Delivery	Between the services actually specified and that actually delivered.
4	Communication	Between the service actually delivered and that externally communicated to customer (e.g., through advertisements).
5	Perception	Between the service quality perceived and that expected by the customer.

It can also be represented as a flow chart as is adopted by Brogowicz et al. (1990) which is termed as the 'gap' model of service delivery. Brown et al. (1990) have also attempted to study the difference between providers and consumers perception of service quality as shown in Table below.

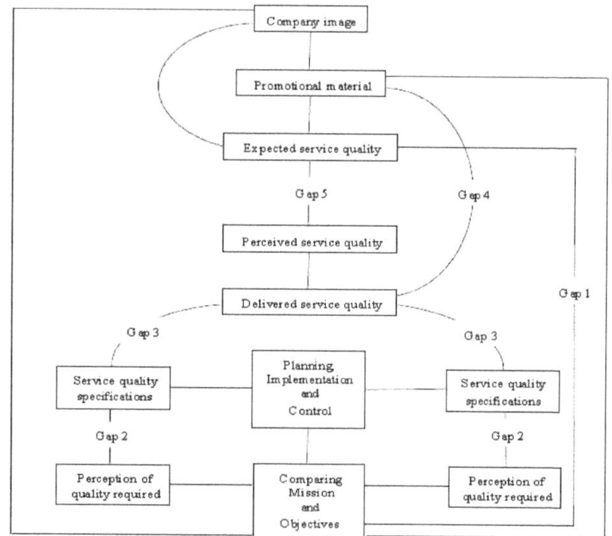

Figure I

Sl.	Designation	Location
1	Professionalism and Skills	Customers see the service providers as knowledgeable and able to solve their problems in a professional way.
2	Attitudes and Behaviours	Customers perceive a genuine, friendly concern for them and their problems.
3	Access and Flexibility	Customers feel that they have easy, timely access and that the service provider is prepared to adjust to their needs.
4	Reliability and Trustworthiness	Customer can trust the service provider to keep promises and act in their best interests.
5	Recovery	Customers know that immediate corrective action will be taken if anything goes wrong.
6	Reputation and Credibility	Customers believe that brand image stands for good performance and accepted values.

Among the numerous reasons identified for the existence of service gap a few notable ones are:

- When top management does not give employees any priority or when they have wrong priorities;
- When middle managers and front line employees are not empowered to make appropriate corrective decision on the spot;
- When the environment or structure of the organisation does not encourage innovation and creativity;
- When top management is complacent; and
- When top management has lost control of one of the gaps – either gap 3 (delivery) or gap 4 (communication) as is shown in the flow chart (Figure).

In order to ensure quality in tourism operations the service provider has to fill in all the gaps.

Chapter-4

MANAGING TOUR OPERATIONS – I (In-house Operations – Inbound and Use of Technology)

Q1. Define what presentation is and describe the types of sale presentations.

Ans. Formal and pre-arranged meeting, usually at a customer's place (or at a neutral premises, such as a hotel) where a salesperson or a sales team presents detailed information (often including live demonstration) about a product or product-line.

A presentation is a commitment by the presenter to help the spectators to do something for solving a problem. An interesting thing to note is that in a presentation commitments are made by the presenter and the audiences are making judgements, simultaneously. The presenter advocates and the audience evaluates, to render a verdict. In terms of content and structure, presentations and speeches have a good deal in common with formal reports – many of them are a oral version of the written document.

Typically, all sales people use one of the following types of sales presentations:

(1) Canned Presentation: Canned presentations are those presentations where text of the presentation is carefully worded, tested and finally written down. While making a presentation, each salesperson is expected to memorise it and strictly follow the contents in the defined order.

The specific advantages of this technique are that one can finish the presentation in a short time and still have a successful close. The other advantage of this method is that it requires lesser time in training the field sales personnel and is most commonly used in non-technical product selling.

The disadvantage of such technique is that the prospect has limited participation. He or she might view it as a high pressure selling and defer taking a purchase decision.

(2) Planned Presentation: It is no doubt carefully planned and organised but still it has a personal touch of the individual making the presentation. In this method, the training department provides just a format and the individual salesperson then writes explanations, descriptions and illustrations.

The advantage of this presentation method is that it appears more conversational and less formal, as the salesperson is using his or her own wordings. As a result, in this presentation method the prospect also gets involved and the prospect's doubts and questions can be carefully handled.

(3) Audio-Visual Presentation: For some presentations the salespersons heavily depend on the Audio Visual (AV) aids. These aids range from charts, slides, video films, prototypes, computer based presentations to the use of actual product. In advertising industry and computer software industry, such presentation methods are used. In these presentations the speaker or the salesperson takes the back seat and the prospect's attention remains centered around the AV aids.

Such aids are typically used, not only to gain the attention but in the absence of these aids it might be difficult to explain or demonstrate the product or service. Web sites on the internet, for example, can be termed as the most sophisticated of these presentations. Hotels and tour operators are now progressively using these methods.

(4) Problem Solving Presentation: This is a two-step presentation method. The first stage is to study the individual prospect's need and the second is suggesting a proposition. Thus, helping the prospect to solve the problem. Such method is commonly used in the insurance sector where the insurance agent asks the prospect about the requirements and accordingly, he or she proposes a specific policy, its advantages and benefits. Selling of conference facilities is another example. Similar methods are also used in management consultancy assignments relating to all functions or high-tech customised products.

Here, we must consider the fact that all types of presentations basically consist of four parts:

(i) **Opening or Introduction:** The introduction of a presentation decides whether you can catch your audience's attention and arouse their interest. The introduction should be brief, stating the purpose and build a focus for your presentation.

(ii) **Body:** The body of a presentation should centre around a selected few important points (3-4). Try not to deviate from these points and read the body language of your audiences, know whether your audience has lost interest. For example, if your audience is yawning or looking everywhere but at you, then you have most certainly lost your audience interest. Audio and visual aids are/ can be used to provide clarification. In the presentations, try to infuse humour and share your experiences to ensure that the presentation does not become boring or monotonous.

(iii) **Ending:** A final summing up is done to further clarify the presentation points but new ideas should not be introduced in this stage. Summing up must cover the specific actions to occur and who would be responsible for doing what.

(iv) **Question and Answer:** A question and answer session facilitates interaction and gives a chance to clarify about your product or service and also emphasise on its benefits. Some speakers answer questions during their presentation while others prefer the questions to the very end of their presentation. Nevertheless questions and answers are an integral part of any presentation.

Q2. Explain different steps of negotiation, and describe the various skills required for each step.

Ans. Negotiating is a procedure of getting the best terms, once the other side starts to act on their interest.

Negotiation involves movement of both the parties. Thus, in a negotiation we must have somewhere to "move from" and somewhere to "move to". We move from our ideal position to a settlement point that is acceptable to both parties. Our opponent also does exactly the same. It is the relative bargaining strength and skill of the negotiators that decides the position of this settlement point.

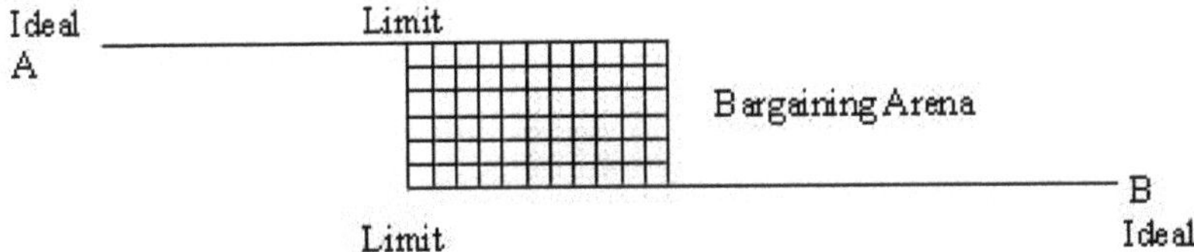

This sample in Figure is static. Negotiation in reality however, is a dynamic process. As the negotiation proceeds, both the sides have to review and modify their limits.

If you look at the above continuum in the context of sales process as a salesperson your ideal position is to sell your product at a maximum benefit while from the customer's angle the ideal position might be to get all the benefits at a much lower price. As the sales process moves, both of you are likely to move from ideal positions and reach a mutually agreeable state if the transaction has to take place.

The negotiating process, for understanding purpose is broken down into the steps through which the negotiations will go if an agreement is to be reached. However, please keep in mind that this is not a rigid order, and the time and attention devoted to different step varies.

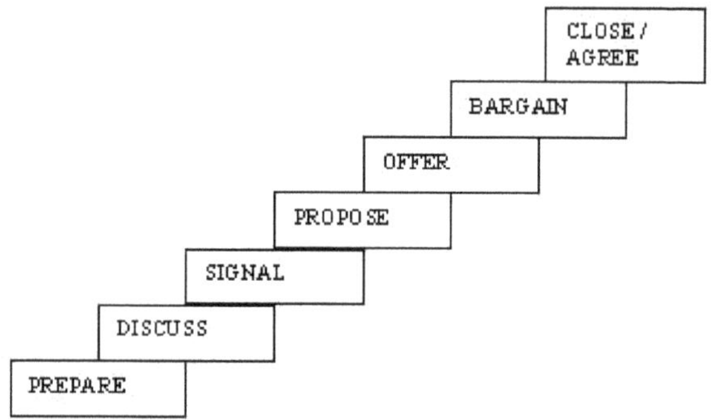

However, it is essential for you to appreciate the importance of each stage, irrespective of the sequence in which they may take place. Table summaries each of these studies.

Step		What you should do
1	Preparing	- Have you decided your objectives? - Have you prioritised them? - Are they realistic? - What are you opponent's objectives? - Do you have information regarding buyer attitudes, personalities, assumptions etc.? - Is your strategy simple and flexible? - In a group negotiation, have each members tasks been clearly defined?
2	Discussion	- Always try to avoid interrupting, talking too much, using sarcasm and threats. - Practice listening, and summarizing.
3	Signaling	- Is your signal generating some movement? - What signals have you made? - If your signals have been ignored, have you tried rewording them? - Are you listening attentively for your opponents' signals?
4	Proposing	- What is the language you are using to convey your proposal? - Have you itemized your proposal? - While receiving a proposal ensure that you do not interrupt it.
5	Offer	- Before making an offer review your opponents and your own objectives. - How can your offer meet all/some of your opponents inhibitions/objectives? - Have you considered all the possible variables in your offer?
6	Bargaining	- Everything must be conditional. - Decide what you require in exchange for your concessions. - Keep all unsettled issues linked.
7	Closing and Agreeing	Decide where you intend to stop trading. - What type of close are you going to use? - Always list the agreement in detail. - If the agreement is oral, always send a written note to your opponent, as soon as possible after the meeting.

(1) Prepare: What you do, or don't, before you arrive at the negotiating table will become evident when you get to negotiations. If you are not fully prepared you can only react to events, you cannot lead them. In the preparation phase you define what needs to be achieved and also decide how it will be achieved. As a negotiator you must know what you want in the short-term and what in the long-term. You must be aware of your opponents expectations and environment. For easy understanding we can sub-divide preparation under a number of key headings: objectives, information, concessions, strategy and tasks:

(i) **Objectives:** The first priority in preparation is to decide your objectives as everything else will follow this. Once you decide your objectives, you must assign relative priorities and question how realistic they are. If your objectives are clearly unattainable you are not likely to gain anything from negotiation. Once you decide your objectives, these also become your criteria for measuring whether the negotiation has been a "success" or a "failure". The first step in deciding objectives is to make a list of all your objectives. The objectives set in any negotiation are only fixed at a given moment of time. Circumstances, people, information, tourist season and so many other factors can alter the objectives and their ranking. After you have listed down all the objectives you can classify them into three categories:

- Like to get,
- Intend to get, and
- Must get.

Relating this step to the sales process is very important for a sales manager/person for then only you decide your call objectives before you meet the customer and categorise them. For example, you are the sales representative of a hotel which has 350 rooms inclusive of all room types such as Single, Double, Deluxe, Suite, etc. And daily, during the off season from a particular travel agency you may:

- Like to get : 30 rooms at 25% profit margin
- Intend to get : 25 rooms at 20% profit margin
- Must get : 20 rooms at 17% profit margin

(ii) **Information:** To establish and prioritize your objectives realistically, considerable amount of information is required. The person with the best information in a negotiation carries a lot of power. After you collect all the information, decide which information to use and which not to use. After deciding your sales objective the more information you can gather about your customer in terms of his or her personality, likes and dislikes, past usage pattern, etc. the easier it will be for you to plan a strategy to deal with him or her. In case of dealing with an organisation it is better to know the organisation's nature of business, business partners and likely expectation from your company and so on.

(iii) **Strategy:** Strategy, as a separate step, will be discussed in detail later in this Unit. However, you must keep in mind that in preparation phase your strategy will need to be mapped out. Thus, the framework or game plan you need to follow to achieve your objectives must be clear. Always ensure that your strategy is not too inflexible. It should be able to respond to developments within the negotiation. Thus, at any stage of negotiation, if you feel that the strategy is not working, you must be able to modify it.

(iv) **Tasks:** In the day-to-day minor negotiations we act as an individual rather than as a member of a team. However, in more important negotiations both the groups involved are likely to have more than one member. In such situations where the group has more than one member it becomes very essential that each member's role and the tasks that he or she has to do are clearly defined and explained. Many times when you are calling a major customer, you may visit him or her as a team from your company. At such meetings it is important that everyone in your team knows what exactly his or her role is and what he or she is going to say during negotiations.

(2) Discussion or Arguing: The second step in the process of negotiation is the discussion or arguing.When the parties involved in negotiation first meet each other, they are aware of the conflict of issues between them. In the instance where the parties have not met each other before this they are most wary of each other. Thus, during the opening phase of the negotiation the atmosphere tends to be very tense.

The discussion step is a major opportunity as you can gain all kind of information regarding the other party's behaviour, intentions and objectives. To gather more and more useful information about your opponent, however you must avoid the habit of interrupting your opponent.

As is normally seen when emotions are charged up, most of us make certain threats, not necessarily intending to carry them out. The most natural reaction to a threat from either side is a counter threat from the other party. In such a situation during a negotiation both the parties may end up with mutual exchange of sanctions. Thus it becomes very critical, that as a party involved in negotiation you depict constructive behaviour. But the problem is, how to show constructive behaviour?

The most important thing, here, is to listen more than you talk. Your positive listening must be supported and followed by positive talking behaviour. The technique for doing this is to ask open questions which will encourage your opponent to explain and elaborate his or her views and ideas.

When the discussions are in progress, one of the factors that will determine the outcome is how well you can send signals. Both the parties involved need to move from their ideal state to mutually acceptable state. The parties involved in the negotiations use sanctions and incentives to ensure movement towards their ideal state.

(3) Signaling Behaviour: When you are involved in negotiations, the way to handle concessions with confidence is to develop skills in signaling behaviour. A good negotiator always tests how strong is his or her opponent's apparent stonewall position. This is the same situation which any salesperson recognizes when he or she is facing objections from the customers. The first thing that a good saleperson does in such a situation is to test whether the objection is real or false. So he or she will ask the customer, " If I was able to overcome this problem, would you be prepared to buy?" For a real objection the customers answer to above question is yes. With the help of signals the parties involved in negotiations indicate their willingness to negotiate.

(i) **What is a Signal?:** The dictionary defines signal as a message. For any message to convey the meaning it has to be interpreted correctly by the receiver. Signals are qualifications placed on a statement of a position. Thus, instead of saying 'I will never agree to your demands' you may say "In the present form your demands are unacceptable to me". A signal is expected to lead to movement.

(ii) **How to Signal?:** For signals to convey message effectively, it is essential that the parties involved in the negotiations are listening to each other. What normally happens is that as both the parties are focusing on their issues, many a times they will miss the signals and prolong the argument. If you are not listening to what your opponent is saying and how he or she is saying it, you will inevitably miss the signals. However, there are many situations during negotiation when you may want to consciously miss a signal. Consciously missing a signal requires a different skill.

During a deadlock, if you are willing to negotiate a solution, you can try to break the argument by signaling or responding positively to signals sent by your opponent. Remember, the method to signal is by adding qualifications to your statements. For example, 'It is not a **normal** practice over here to give credit', '**everything** you are suggesting cannot be accepted', etc.

(iii) **What to do when your opponent ignores the signal?:** If there is no response to your signals from your opponent, you must analyse first, whether he or she has missed the signal or is he or she intentionally ignoring the signal. If your opponent has missed the signal you can either repeat it verbatim or in a modified form. 'Everything you are suggesting cannot be accepted in its current form' can be repeated as 'you cannot expect us to accept everything you are suggesting in its current form.' After having tried a signal, repeat it in different forms, and on receiving a response to any one of the signals from your opponent, you must decide whether you want to move out of discussion or more importantly whether negotiations are possible in current circumstances.

(4) Proposing: Discussions, opinions and prejudices cannot be negotiated, only proposals can. When an argument is prolonged, the way out is by a signal which leads to a proposal. In the context of negotiation a proposal is an offer which establishes a realistic opening position.

When you are presenting an initial proposal, you would most likely state your ideal position, and your language will effect the firmness of your position, 'I had expected much better service.'

When you present a secondary proposal, you are trying to initiate a move forward to common ground. Thus, the language used for secondary proposals in most cases is tentative 'I may look into the possibility of considering this'.

(i) **How to Present a Proposal?:** The best way to present a proposal is to keep it separate from reasoning and justification. The reasoning must be reserved for only those cases where it is absolutely necessary. The party that puts the proposal first usually gains a upper position in the negotiation as after having put the proposal, it can always seek a response, "Is my proposal acceptable?'

(ii) **How to Receive a Proposal?:** To effectively receive a proposal, you must curb two common behaviour patterns: interrupting and instant rejection. When you interrupt a proposal you are likely to miss something which was yet to be proposed, as very often experienced negotiators will tag a concession at the end of a proposal.

The other important behaviour to control is its instant rejection. Even when the opponent's proposal is absolutely unacceptable to you, treat the proposal with some respect. Listen carefully to the complete proposal and then ask questions to clarify the points that may not be clear to you. If you are well prepared then reply to the proposal and in case you need some time to finalise, ask for an adjournment. The main purpose of an adjournment is to review and assess progress against the set objectives. The actual number and frequency of adjournments depends upon the practice of negotiators involved. The most useful skill in handling proposals and counter-proposals is the summarising skill. Regular summarising of issues keeps both the parties concentrated to issues.

(5) Packaging the Offer: Offer moves the negotiations into the bargaining arena. But before the bargaining begins, one should package the offer, suitably. What is an offer? In the context of negotiations, an offer is considered an activity in response to the opening moves of the negotiation. When you present an offer, you present the variables in a form which more clearly match the other party's interests and inhibitions. For example, a sales executive of a hotel to the travel agent – "I will give 10% extra discount on the special rate". Before presenting the offer you must think carefully and creatively about all the possible variables.

(6) Bargaining: Bargaining is about exchange – you give up something and gain something. This is the most intense phase of negotiation.

The single most important rule of bargaining is to make all propositions and concessions, conditional. Thus, while bargaining you give away nothing, absolutely nothing for free. You always use the big "IF".

"If you agree to X, I will agree to Y".

Another point to keep in mind is to put your bargaining proposals as statements and not as questions "If you inform the discount, and promise to deliver in seven days, then I will process the order'.

While during the proposal step you make tentative offers. 'I will consider,' I will look into' etc., in the bargaining step you firm up your proposals and become more positive 'If you do X', I will do Y'.

Very often in negotiation, a party will present a list of demands, objections, requirements, etc., followed by the logical suggestion that each item is dealt with one at a time. If other party presents such an idea, don't agree to such a demand. Always try to ensure that you keep all the issues in dispute linked. If you agree to negotiate item by item the other party has good chances of squeezing you. However, this depends on the situation.

(7) Closing and Agreeing: The purpose of closing is to lead both the parties to a final agreement. Thus, closing must be credible. Your closing package must meet enough of your opponents needs to be acceptable. Two common types of closes used during negotiations are concession close and summary close.

(i) **Concession Close:** When you use a concession close, you terminate the bargaining step by offering a concession to secure agreement. For example, a sales executive to the travel agency executive looking after the conference delegation, "We will provide rooms on room plus breakfast basis, at the rates you asked for. And we will also provide the morning tea and snacks during the conference, daily, free of cost but only for this delegation."

(ii) **Summary Close :** Summary close terminates the bargaining step by summarising everything that has been agreed upto then, highlighting the concessions that the customers have secured from your side, and emphasising the benefits of agreeing to what is on the table.

For example, Sales executive to the travel agency executive looking after the conference delegation, "The rates are the best you can get. As you know, we are providing rooms at the rate you asked for and that too on room plus breakfast basis. Plus we will also provide morning tea and snacks during the conference, free of cost. Plus, we are also providing space, table, phone lines and other facilities along with tea and lunch for your team of two people stationed in our hotel for handling this delegation. And we will see that check-in and check-out takes the least possible time of your delegation."

Agreeing is the last step towards which both the parties have been working. The purpose of closing is to secure agreement to what is on offer. It is of utmost importance that both or all the parties involved rate absolutely clear on what they have agreed to before they leave the table.

(8) Deadlock: We have seen all the steps of the negotiation process. During any of the steps, negotiations could enter deadlock. A deadlock stops the negotiation process. Deadlock has a price. Its most obvious price is the fact that the time spent in trying to negotiate a deal becomes a dead loss to the organisation, if the deadlock is irresolvable. Deadlocks occur in many negotiations despite the best efforts of the negotiators. Some deadlocks are temporary, others can be permanent. The way to handle a deadlock is to keep your emotions, prejudices out of the issue and work towards finding some common objectives. Your basic intention should be to get negotiation process moving again, so as to enable a solution, acceptable to both parties.

❑❑❑

Chapter-5

MANAGING TOUR OPERATIONS – II (Field Operations – Inbound and Out-bound)

Q1. How would you manage outbound tours ? Does the requirement for outbound tour differ from inbound tour ? Support your answer with suitable example.

Ans. Outbound tourism refers to a Visits by the residents of a country to another country - ,for example when an Indian citizen, Mr. Ram goes to America to see Hollywood , he is an outbound tourist for India.

This section specializes in providing services to only those passengers who intend travelling abroad. In order to perform a variety of jobs, it can be divided into following small sections:

(1) Documentation Section: To travel abroad one requires procuring a number of documents and fulfil a set of formalities. This section, therefore, focuses upon these formalities and documents required for all types of foreign travel. Any person wanting to go abroad shall have to come into contact with the documentation section of the travel agency/tour operations department. It is only after asking the reason of visit you can and shall advice him/her about the documents needed for obtaining the required visa of the country of visit or for any other approval like that of RBI or Income Tax Office.

The formalities and the documents needed for travel abroad differ according to the purpose of visit. There are various reasons for travelling abroad – tourists for higher education, business, medical treatment, immigration, etc. In each case the formalities and the supporting documents differ not only from country to country but from the point of view of motives of travel also.

(2) Visa Section: This section keeps all the information for the formalities involved in obtaining visa for different countries. The staff collects and endorses passports on behalf of passengers and delivers them to passengers much in advance from the date of journey.

(3) Reservation Section: This is another important section which deals with the reservation of transport and hotel accommodation. The staff in this section has to be well conversant with all the airlines' timetables, airfares for different sectors and hotel accommodations, types and tariffs at most visited destinations.

After taking note of all the details of the programme information is recorded by them on a specially printed sheet of paper. Thereafter a suitable travel plan is drawn giving suitable flight connections with arrival/departure timing and places of stay. It also makes an approximation of the cost for staying and the airfare. After the approval of the travel plan, a finally typed copy is given to the passenger for his reference. This is known as itinerary.

After getting the itinerary approved the reservation section contacts the concerned airlines and asks for seats as per the itinerary. The concerned airline will also be given a copy of the full programme of the passenger because it will also send reservation messages to its concerned officers for the onward flight confirmation as per the programme. On obtaining all the confirmations, the airline informs the agent that all the onward reservations are ready. On receipt of this information the agent issues its voucher drawn on the airlines asking them to issue their tickets in favour of the passenger as per the details of the flight given in the voucher. Some of the important contents of voucher may include:

(i) Name of the Passenger,
(ii) Place to be Visited,
(iii) Date,
(iv) Flight Number,
(v) Time,
(vi) RBI Permit Number,
(vii) Passport Number,
(viii) Applicable Fare, and
(ix) Agent Code Number.

After receiving this voucher the airline issues the tickets. The ticket is sent to the agent who crosschecks it and after complete satisfaction hands it over to the passenger. Thus, it is seen that you have to provide a number of services to the passenger for which no extra amount is charged. The passenger gets the benefit of guidance and services from you. You must acknowledge the fact that in your absence he/she would have had to waste a lot of time, energy and money.

Another feature of outbound tours is selling the packages of the inbound tour operators of other countries. There are few big companies who develop their own outbound packages and the product designing in such cases involves all steps that are necessary for developing a tour package. However, when you act as a seller of others, you must ensure that the package actually has in terms of services all that which has been promised. Fam trips, linkages and experience help in this regard. Such a precaution is must because it is you who is selling to the tourist. If anything goes wrong the tourist will hold you responsible and the same will be the case in a consumer court.

Inbound Tour: Inbound tourism refers to Visits to a country by non-resident of that country - for example, when A American citizen, Mr. Sam comes to India to see the Taj Mahal, he is an inbound tourist for India.

A good impression, in the very beginning of the visit, will put everyone in the right mood towards an overall success. Reverse to this situation would make them feel that they have committed a mistake by choosing this country as a destination and they start foreseeing a lot of problems all during their stay. This could mean that they are likely to make complaints even over small matters, and it could also mean that they will refuse to buy the extra services which otherwise would have contributed to your company's financial gains. Hence, properly prepared, planned and well-conducted transfers of groups will ensure a smooth and happy start. While doing so train your staff to always put themselves in the clients' shoe and how would they feel after a long flight when they are not only tired but they may also be dehydrated (as a result of the physical effects of flying, and of drinking alcohol on the flight which exaggerates this effect). They may be suffering from the change of climate from their country to yours. (A North European coming to South Asia in January could be experiencing a difference of as much as 45 to 50oC which requires a little adjustment). They are often nervous, for there is a fear of a foreign culture, foreign food, foreign people of different races and colours, of getting lost, ill, or robbed, and who knows what others fears! Of course, you can also look at these fears in a more positive way and can be regarded as part of the challenge, the excitement, or travelling abroad. After -all your clients did choose to come to you. Therefore, you must train your staff to apprise the tourist(s) being comfortable and safe. Once this is achieved atmosphere of noisy and hot airport bureaucracy and rudeness of many immigration and customs officials, the delay for that luggage, and the inadequacy of the trolleys can also be overlooked by them because what clients expect from you at this stage is:

- feel safe and secure,
- satisfy physical needs,
- belong with others, and
- have their status recognised.

Everything you plan before, during or after their transfer must centre around fulfilment of these needs. You should also consider whether your clients actually need you to conduct this transfer for them? He/she may not, since most adults are capable of finding their way to wherever they wish to go. It may take them longer, especially if there are language problems, and it may be less comfortable, more expensive, and slower to do it themselves but still they need you because you can do transfers for them more cheaply, more quickly, more comfortably, than they can themselves, and you can also provide for all those personal needs which are listed above. If you are unable to manage all this you are as good as those tourists in arranging all this for themselves. Clients will soon realise this and your business will evaporate. Now let us look at what steps you shall take as a manager to ensure that all goes well and the clients' needs are met. In fact, several days before pre-arrival day you should crosscheck:

- that required/requested kind of transport has been booked, i.e., booked vehicle should be the right kind of vehicle for the purpose.
- that your staff is using the most appropriate transport for your clients. Clients may have requested air conditioned vehicle or they may have been carrying a lot of luggage so that a larger vehicle or even a second vehicle especially for the baggage may be needed. (This particularly applies to active special interest groups like divers, climbers, trekkers, and campers).
- the transport arranged by your staff must be reliable, safe, well maintained and clean. The driver must be briefed as to exactly where the transport will be located in the airport terminal building and how escort can locate it. You must check if a voucher is required for transport and hotel must be released by you well in advance and must ensure that there vouchers are prepared for all items and after rate agreed. If there is need for some cash for payment of porterage of luggage then you must assess the required amount and release the cash. Ensure that your staff has informed the transport company about the number of passengers and bags expected and other relevant details.
- As a good manager/supervisor it is your responsibility to ensure that hotel rooms in required numbers shall be made available on arrival and you shall also advise the hotel front office and house keeping about what time the clients will actually be arriving in the hotel so that the housekeeping department is ready for them (this is especially true in the case of very late arrivals).

Not only this you should also apprise your staff about other needs of your clients.

You must always brief the escort to collect and carry information on:

- Flight number;
- Name list;
- Details of transport, transport voucher;
- Hotels' name and address, rooming list and hotel voucher;
- Together with any special details such as the nature of the group, difficulties with mobility, VIPs, etc.; and

- Greeting/sign board (individual tourist's placard giving name of the tourist, country coming from or company he/she is representing, etc.).

In some cities where there is a long transfer between airport and city there is a representative who meets at the airport and then despatches the group to the hotel where another representative awaits. In such cases it becomes important for you to arrange for both. In an identical briefing, but, of course, one who receives at the airport has the transport vouchers and one who escorts them to hotels will have the hotel vouchers. In such a system you need to develop proper communication systems between both the employees and try to provide both of them mobile phones so that both of them can update each other about the movements of the tour ist(s).

It is for you to develop a culture of checks and rechecks among your staff. For example, before reaching the airport they should call the airline and establish the Actual time of arrival. This is possible only when the aircraft has actually left its departure point. Advise them not be persuaded by the scheduled time of arrival which can be widely different due to technical or non-technical reasons.

If there is a substantial change to the timings ask them always to advise the transport company and the hotel of changes, accordingly. You must ensure that your transfer staff has reached at the airport before the passengers come out of the waiting hall. Tell by your experiences for how long it may take for passengers to come out of the immigration cell. Try to provide your staff an airside pass only then he/she enter the customs hall assisting and greeting passengers. In some airports where this is not allowed because of security concerns you must apprise your staff of the same so that they shouldn't commit any thing of this sort and while doing transfers they must position themselves in public/visitor's gallery immediately outside the customs hall closely indicating their guest's/group leader's name.

- You should take precautions at this point of time to gain first impression for your company since you will not get another chance to repair your impressions,
- Your staff should be clean, neat, and very well groomed (Use the personality factor),
- Your staff should be wearing a badge which identifies him/her as the official in charge of your clients; and
- If possible your staff can wear a uniform since this also helps your client to easily recognise and trust the staff deputed.

In short, you must equip your airport transfer boy/girl with the following material ready for use:

- Badge,
- Uniform as prescribed,
- Greeting board,

- Name list,
- Clipboard and pen,
- Mobile phone or phone card or coins,
- Tips or voucher for porters,
- Transport vouchers,
- Hotel vouchers,
- Welcome packs and/or gifts,
- Hotel registration cards, and
- Smile of the escort.

Certain other aspects to be taken care of include:

(1) Passengers' Identification: You must train your staff to greet tourists cheerfully and briefly welcome them, and tick them off on his/her list (for the purpose of security and status), ask them to wait in the waiting lounge so as to allow all members of the group to assemble. In case, if he/she finds that someone is missing, immediately ask the airport information service to announce:

- Name of missing passenger,
- Name of tour group,
- Place arrived from,
- Easily identifiable meeting point, and
- Ensure this announcement is in the language the passenger speaks.

On rare occasions when the passenger does not appear, your staff must be apprised of procedures as to immediately check with the airline that whether the group was in fact on board the flight or not. If not, there is no need to wait. If so, then your staff is required to repeat the public announcement and shall also leave a written note at the information point giving advice to the passenger about how to catch up with the group. You must advise your transfer staff to wait for at least 30 minutes and then continue with the transfer. It is advisable that at all stages of tour your staff keep the other passengers informed of the reasons for the delay (This reassures them that you are doing a careful job).

If any passenger reports loss or damaged baggage in the customs/baggage areas your staff shall be trained to fill forms for tracing/ replacing the bags obtained from the airline staff. This is where your airside pass would of great help. Your staff at this juncture shall reassure the passengers, who feel very scared under this situation and may become very upset. Make sure that the airline gives the passenger copies of all forms filled in and that these are carefully kept by the clients as they will be required for insurance claims. The airlines are responsible for finding and forwarding lost bags and fixed rates of compensation are payable to help with the cost of toiletries, and other essentials when bags are lost or delayed. In such cases your staff shall offer themselves to go with the client for this essential shopping.

Another critical situation comes when at any point of time your staff has to leave the clients to attend to another matter advise them to always "signpost". This means that should not just disappear but they explain therein where they are going and why. Failing to do this can lead to chaos amongst the group members. Examples could be "please stay here I am going to check on the coach" or "I will be back in 10 minutes, I am going to help with that damaged bag".

When your staff has all the passengers, and all their bags are accounted for, he/she should lead the group to the vehicle holding the welcome notice high so that they can follow them through a crowd. Go steadily, so that all can keep up, and talk to the passengers in a welcoming manner about their journey, etc. It is advisable that you should instruct your staff to take care of group members while crossing roads. Before boarding the vehicle your staff shall also ensure that each person checks/is requested to identify their own bags been loaded. Usually, the loading will be done by the porters or the driver but they cannot be expected to know which bag belongs to whom. Before moving off welcome the group again, saying your name clearly and checking the number of passengers present is still correct. When your driver is driving a group to the hotel you should advise him to introduce himself as well the name of the hotel and tell the group the approximate driving time that may take to reach there.

(2) Departure Transfers: Tourists who arrive in groups or as individuals are required to go through transfer procedure once again, i.e., the departure transfer. The departing experience of a client is as crucial as arrival transfer for your company's image. Departure transfer for your clients is to be handled very professionally by your staff. Like the arrival transfer it starts some days beforehand. Within 72 hours after arrival all scheduled seats for the next sector should be reconfirmed. This means that you should have gathered up all the tickets and done this for your clients. Beware, there are just a few airlines which have different requirements such as "reconfirm within 72 hours of departure" and failure to comply can lose clients their seats. Get to know your local situation. You are supposed to act professionally while

handling/supervising such transfers. For instance, each and every client must be advised in writing one day before of their flight time and date and pick up time from the hotel. This can be achieved by putting a notice on the tour notice board, or you can leave a letter for each client with reception. (If you do not put this in writing there is a risk that a client who misses the flight can blame you.) Details of any departure tax payable should be included. Once again, you need to reconfirm transport and voucher arrangements with the transport company and double check that there is no change in the flight time. You need to establish and inform how much in advance before the departure clients should settle their extra bills at reception. Computerised accounts of hotels can usually issue bills just before departure unless the group is very large, but some properties prefer this to be done a night before.

On departure day you shall advise your staff to follow the departure transfer checklist (given below) which is essentially the same as for the arrival transfer. Remember that the customers' needs are the same, i.e., full attention. He or she may again be nervous and unsure but by now has developed trust in you and should be easier to direct.

Departure Transfer Checklist:

- Brief clients in writing and in advance,
- Brief hotel and porters to be ready,
- Be at hotel early,
- Ask reception if everyone has paid extras,
- Gather up clients, phone rooms of those who do not appear,
- Load bags (each client to confirm),

Remind clients to:

- pay extras,
- return keys,
- empty safe deposits, and
- have passports and tickets in hand luggage.
- Load passengers,
- Depart for airport,
- On route explain procedure at airport,
- Explain what facilities there are airside (toilets? Post office? Duty-free? Bars? Café?),
- Drive as close as possible to check in area,
- Before leaving bus wish them a safe and happy journey home and that they will come back soon.

Sound as if you mean it,

- While saying goodbye some passengers may offer small tips and gifts. Thank for these but

NEVER solicit them,

- Assist with getting porters/trolleys,
- Assist with check in procedures/airport tax paying, etc.,
- Escort to security and passport control,
- When all have gone airside you can leave but not before, and
- If there is a delay before the clients have gone airside you are still responsible for them.

(3) Other Areas for Supervision in Inbound Tour Operations: Tourism is a very sensitive industry as it deals with people and their holidays. In the preceding sections various aspects that are necessary were mentioned for making the customer feel comfortable.

However, certain other aspects should also be taken into account.

- As a tour operator you must manage your finances well.
- As a tour operator, besides having proper product knowledge, you must also have a proper understanding about the functioning

and role of each organisation (like airline, hotel, surface transport, Government department, such as, Archaeological Survey, Ministry of Environment, etc.). He or she should also analyse the options available and work out contingency plans.

- You, as well as your employees in a tour operation company should always be prepared to react to any sudden development (strikes, health problems, political upheaval, non-availability of hotels or airline seats, etc.) to handle such situations, you should train your staff to take on the spot decision to offer solutions.
- Increasing use of technology has considerably changed the nature of operations management. However, computers, fax machines and even telephone systems also keep breaking down (e.g., power cuts, etc.). Hence, it is important that you should also train your employees in manual systems as it comes handy in times of crisis.
- Market research, market segmentation, understanding the tourist markets, tourist profiles, etc. are essential for achieving success in business and a tour operator must pay considerably attention on these aspects. Besides, proper linkages have to be established with principal suppliers. Preparing attractive brochures, participation in travel marts and travel conventions help the tour operator in increasing business. Many tour operators are also going for straight selling to the customers by putting advertisements in the print as well as electronic media.

Q2. Why is it important to maintain good relations with your suppliers in tour operations business?

Ans. Just like any other industrial operations tour operations largely depend upon the sources of supply. Here the point of difference is that industrial supplies are not visible to the consumer. For example, if you are producing edible oil, the consumer will not come to know who supplies you the raw material but in tourism operation suppliers like airlines, hotels, shopping malls, cultural attractions, all are visible for customers. Moreover, each one of these principal suppliers contributes towards the satisfaction of customers.

These service providers play vital role in your successful operation of tours and you need to develop and manage linkages with these suppliers. You have already been told that there are two areas of operations, i.e., inbound and outbound tour operations. Therefore, for each of these areas linkages work differently because the suppliers are different. In the case of inbound tour operations when you plan to design your product you are required not only to collect complete information on what type of travel products are available in the markets and at what price but also you will have to match the existing products with suitable target market segment.

For example, if you are approached by a group of tourists having interest in Buddhist circuit, you must have complete and authentic information on all the components of this product including the providers of services and costs only then you can price and offer such a package. Here comes the need for developing contacts with the service providers to supply you with accurate information. If possible, conduct a familiarisation tour before taking decisions. Moreover, as a manager, you can negotiate well on various terms and conditions of such purchases when you have developed good rapport with them.

Principal suppliers may include airlines, hotels, transporters, insurance companies, health service providers, conference and convention organisers, shopkeepers/shopping mall owners and many more to complete the list, depending on the nature of the product to be packaged.

On the other hand, in case of outbound tour operations such linkages focus upon overseas suppliers who are also on look out for distributors of their products. You might have seen advertisements of Indian tour operators selling destinations like Singapore, Malaysia, Bangkok, Pattaya, Switzerland, France, Mauritius, Australia, New Zealand and many more at attractive costs. This all has become

possible because of good linkages these tour operators are able to establish with their overseas suppliers. This has resulted in good terms for negotiations for both the parties, i.e., if overseas supplier assures good price you have to commit good volume of business. This forms the core point of difference between your quotations of a package from that of your competitors.

Thus, linkages can play crucial role in making your operations a success or failure. For that reason, you are advised to build up and sustain linkages and contacts with your suppliers both within the country as well as at other destinations.

Chapter-6

MANAGING TOUR OPERATIONS – III (Managing Distribution)

Q1. Explain the role of distribution channels in tourism.

Ans. The distribution decision is primarily concerned with the supply chain's front-end or channels of distribution that are designed to move the product (goods or services) from the hands of the company to the hands of the customer. Obviously when we talk about intangible services the use of the word "hands" is a figurative way to describe the exchange that takes place.

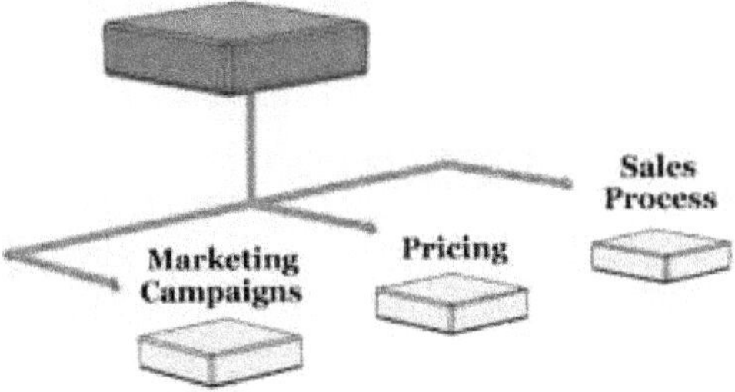

Apart from making the goods or services presented to the end users, distribution means also to make consumers aware of their availability and upgradation from time to time. This necessitates due emphasis on managing the personnel engaged in distributing or channelising the services/products. In return tourists are able to make their tour memorable and purposeful with the help of these channels of distribution. Offering of services in a professional manner has a far -reaching impact on the organisational prosperity and this impact, no doubt can only be created through the skills and professionalism of distributors. For instance, if tourist(s) visit a monument and there is no guide or escort their normal eyes will fail in identifying and feeling the realities related to these historical monuments. With the availability of an efficient guide or escort even language constraints are overcome and the overall impact can be visualised. In tourism your delivery channels have to act as interpreters of your package while promoting it.

Not much time ago tourism industry was posed with the problem of transmission of information about products to interested persons. Today, however, the introduction of computerised reservation systems, sales desk terminals and touch screen has not only simplified but also speeded up the distribution process. Therefore, your role now is just to simplify and rationalise your distribution process or system. Various factors that may influence your distribution system can be:

- **Image of Your Organisation:** It is the most important factor for formulating a sound distribution policy. If the image is positive and fair, your task would be simple, but if you are already facing image problem your task is likely to be quite complicated and complex. It is essential that your products/services are pushed strongly through distribution chains to create the desired image not only for your products/services but also for your company, otherwise survival in the industry would be very difficult.
- **Location of Points of Sale (PoS):** You can very well manage your distribution system if you are able to select sensitive points of sale in order to attract the tourists. These are basically target markets where potential tourists live or work. Therefore, it is important for all tour operators to target these points for creating a favourable image of their products and services.
- **Costs of Distribution:** Cost of distribution is also an important factor in overall policy formulation exercises. It is possible that only after this exercise you decide whether you want to sell your products through travel agents, travel clubs, and other specific organisations. While doing so you shall take into account the commission considerations of intermediaries that you want to involve. While costing for distribution you must also consider staff wages, rents, electricity and water charges, telephone, postage as well as profit margins as per the policy of the company.
- **Users' Perceptions Regarding Products:** The perception of tourists regarding your products/services is also a factor which you should consider while framing the distribution policy. If products are in line with the tastes and preferences of the tourists and are designed well to meet their expectations, your task of promotion and distribution is simplified.
- **Effectiveness of Marketing Efforts:** If marketing efforts by your company are sound then you can formulate a sound distribution policy too and thus, success is nearer. This clearly indicates at

whether you have accorded due priority to the different marketing tools in relation to changing stages of product life cycle or not. If yes, nothing can stop you from achieving your objectives and if not, you are advised to do so before drafting your distribution policy.

Thus, these factors mentioned above not only govern the intensity of success of your organisation's distribution system but also sustain flow of products on and through right path.

Q2. Discuss four types of sales distribution process in relation to tour operations.

Ans. Distribution Systems combines the right skills with the right platform for the best integrated wholesale and distribution solution. A basic understanding of the distribution structure in tour operations outlines primarily four types of distribution systems, viz.,

(1) One Stage Distribution System: In this system of distribution primary supplier reach directly through their own outlets to consumers. In this context you will find "Do it yourself" model of **Douglas Foster** is very interesting in which hotels feed hotel directories and travel timetables are fed by airlines.

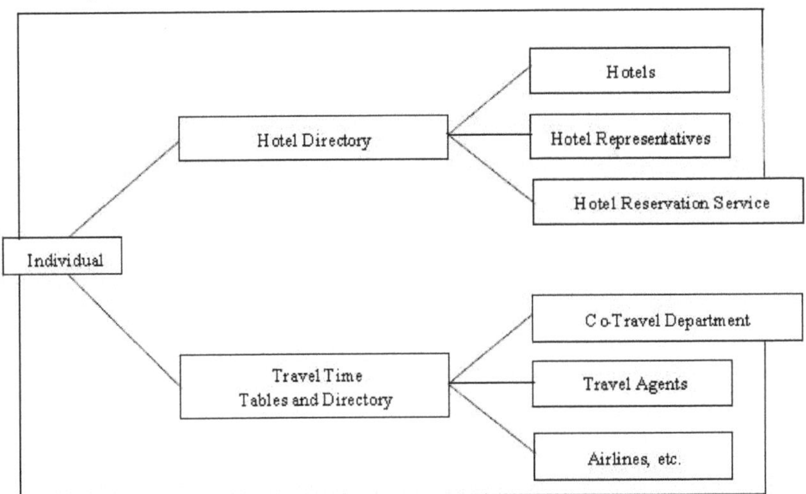

(2) Two Stage Distribution System: This involves a single middleman between supplier and traveller, i.e., a travel agent with advantage of buying other products for and getting a single bill for all services.

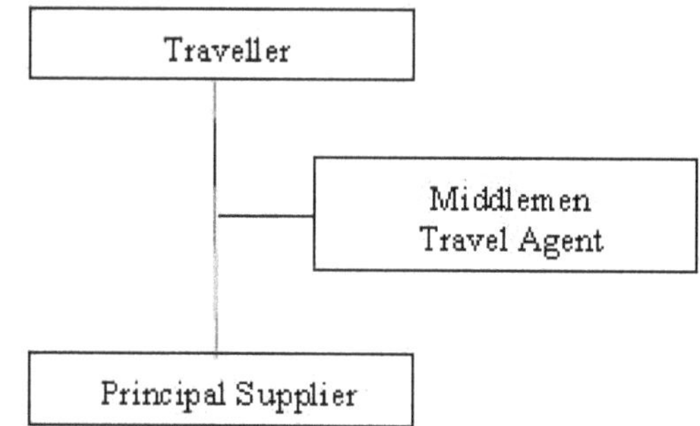

(3) Three Stage Distribution Systems: It involves two middlemen, i.e., a retailer and a wholesaler or a tour operator.

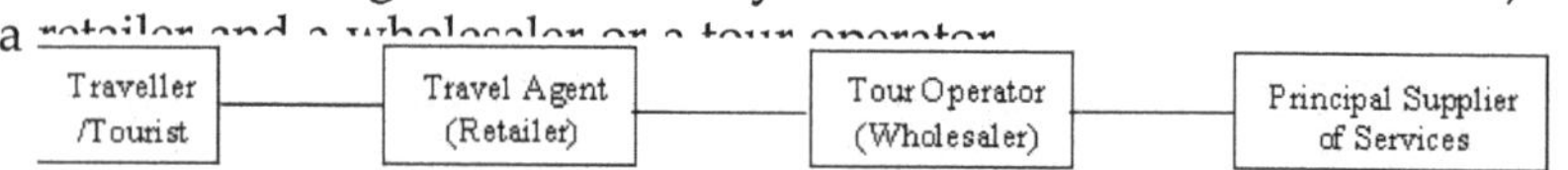

(4) Four Stage Distribution System: In this distribution process you have additional middlemen known as Speciality Chancellor instrumental in developing tour packages, e.g.,

Traveller /Tourist — Travel Agent (Retailer) — Tour Operator (Wholesaler) — Secondary Supplier* — Principal Supplier of Services

* or speciality chancellors, e.g., escorts, guides, etc.

(5) In the present age of automation, technological advancements have particularly revolutionised the selling of tourism products/services. Internet is the word of the day. Today tourists have the access to suppliers through network. Therefore, they are able to get a better deal for the products required by them. Similarly, on the other hand, sellers are also able to display their product and price range for customers to choose from.

Chapter-7

MANAGING A TOUR: ESCORT

Q1. How, as an escort, would you manage a tour?

Or

Discuss the steps involved in packaging a tour.

Ans. Escort is the one who is the guide, philosopher and manager of the tourist as for practically everything the tourist depends on the escort. The role of an escort begins as soon as a tourist arrives at his/her destination. It continues all through his/her stay and ends only with the departure. Unlike a guide, an escort may not be free from his/her responsibilities at any hour of the day. This is because in escorted tours the job also involves looking after facilitation aspects like facilitation at the airports, hotels and city tours, etc. In fact, an escort is responsible for everything that the tourist group requires at the destination.

Besides taking into account certain considerations for escorting purposes one has to prepare for operating the schedules. Certain guidelines may prove useful in this regard.

- Knowledge of the group profile in advance, like the tastes, interests, etc. of the tourists help in this regards. For example, you may have looked at the date of birth of a tourist from the profile and if this date falls during the tour schedule you can surprise the tourist by not only wishing a happy birthday but also offering a gift and converting the occasion into some sort of celebration.
- Normally the escort has the knowledge about the areas to be visited, but a good escort with high professional skills will always update oneself once again about what's going on at the destination. This helps in preparing oneself in advance for making commentaries to the tourists
- A good escort will prepare the tourists in advance for all that has to be encountered during the tour. Yet he/she may keep something to be thrown as special surprises to the tourists.
- The tour escort must have in his basket jokes for the occasions

which can also be used to divert attention if something has gone wrong, e.g., time spent on mending a flat tyre has to be converted into time for amusement rather than leaving it as a boring or irritating wait.

All successful tours tell the same story, i.e., good preparation. Therefore, you are advised to pay attention to the following details at the stage of preparation:

- You must prepare a checklist of all items and details pertaining to the tour. As a result, you will not forget even the minutest item from the list. This will prove to be a successful tool at preparation stage. For example, if you are escorting a tour to a wild life sanctuary or for a trekking, your requirements would be different. If you have prepared your checklist you will not forget to carry each and every item required.
- Details about itinerary, i.e., different routes and places to be covered must be carefully memorised and all events must be planned in such a manner so that they can fit in your itinerary.
- Commentary is yet another factor crucial while escorting the tour. This commentary is advisable to be crisp, informative and delightful, punctuated with humour is the sure key to your success as an escort. At many a times due to wonderful commentaries, escorts are complemented and this promotes your organisation.
- Nevertheless you must plan travel tips which are vital for your group. If not planned carefully these would become pits for you to fall in. In other words, success or failure of your tour largely depends upon travel tips that you give to your group members during the tour period.
- The escort also ensures hiring of good guides as per the requirements of the tourist groups.

Q2. How, as an escort, would handle difficult situations.

Ans. The tour escort should habitually have the force and guts to cope with special situations and accidents. Some of the most frequently encountered situations are:

- **Loss of Money and Passports** is the most common complaint of groups. It is, therefore, advisable for you as an escort to request all group members to deposit their passports with you during the duration of tour. You must also advise them not to carry much of cash with them and to transact most of their business/exchange activities through travellers' cheques or credit cards.
- **Sickness** is yet another situation. When this situation arises you should first see if any of the group member is of some help. In the meantime try and contact nearest medical centre for first aid

treatment.

- **Missing members** is another typical situation of a tour group. Generally such situations occur when visiting a monument, a crowded place or sometimes when a tourist ventures to move on ones own. Such situations can be avoided by requesting the tourists to strictly adhere to the briefings given for the occasion and at the same time you must mention the timings of departure from that particular place so that in case someone has missed the group the person can be back at that time. In certain cases you have to be persuasive but without loosing your cool.
- Though political events, strikes, road blocks, etc. had been there earlier as bottlenecks in smooth tour operations, **terrorism has added an all together new dimension in this regard**. Hence, your escorts need a different kind of training altogether of handling such situations without being panicky and losing confidence.
- In general, the escort should always be prepared to meet uncalled for situations, unexpected challenges/situations and for this experience in the field counts a lot.
- The escort must ensure filling of feedback forms from the tour group and filling his/her own report to the company.

Q3. Describe considerations for An Escort.

Ans. When it comes to escort a tour and manage it, on your part it calls for careful preparation and planning. Hence, the escort has to be equipped for special situations also that may arise from unforeseen circumstances. Though each tour is unique on its own the tour escort should be trained and involved in the planning aspect of the tour. For this knowledge of the following is important:

- Components of the entire tour package, i.e., the destination offered, day itineraries, services included in the package, time schedules, type of accommodations, mode of transports, local guide services, etc.
- Rate of success with similar tours in the past: This would enable a tour escort to analyse which areas created success or where shortcomings have resulted in failure of a particular tour. How shortcomings should be avoided, should be chalked out. Here the reports filed of earlier tour escorts help a lot in planning for new tour operations. It is only after analysing this rate of success and failure as well as reason for the same you can and shall plan your operations.
- Prime motivation for existence of every business activity is to generate profit for the organisation and in this regard tour operations is no exception. However, one has to be extremely

cautious while broadening the scope of the tour in relation to what has been offered in the initial package. The best pricing practice is to include all services and items that are to be charged right at the beginning when the package is sold. Additional services, if any, offered during the tour require extreme caution as regards the tourist getting the feeding that she/he is being fleeced or cheated.

- Ensure that prior information is there for welcoming the tourists at every point of their journey. This will not only help in smooth operations but welcome at every point would give the satisfaction to the tourists that they are being cared for.

Your escort must carry a mobile phone or pager wherein he/she may be contacted in case of any delay or any other emergency at the airport or tourist site.

The itinerary of the group/individual tourist is already fixed, however, a tour escort must live the tour day by day. While doing so he/she must take special care of the following areas:

- **Scheduling:** Scheduling is a procedure by which we try to assure and combine factors with uncertain variables. The focus of scheduling is to look for right place, at right time for the right people and at a right price. As an escort or as a manager, managing a team of escorts, you must apprehend and appreciate the significance of scheduling in your overall planning process. It is through scheduling that you plan target dates and times for successful completion of your assignments. Be it visiting a monument on a particular day which may be a special day, for instance, visiting the Taj on full moon day or visiting Khajuraho temples during Khajuraho festival, you have to schedule it in such a manner that the tour results in a memorable experience for the group.
- **Events:** You should plan attending events on a tour to suit the taste of most of the tourists in the group. However, in doing so the cost factor should be taken into account and also that some may not have an inclination for it. But as an escort managing the show, you must convince them about the relative importance of each event in its cultural, social and economic perspective, leaving it to their judgement whether to attend it or not. Do not compel the tourists.
- **Variables:** An escort should take into consideration the weather, unforeseen, occurrences, transport upsets and some other variables which can play vital role in making any tour a pleasant and memorable experience. If such variables are not considered, losses can be irreparable.

Q4. write how to manage escort services?

Ans. In tour operations, escort has a very specialised meaning. He/she is the one who is the guide, philosopher and manager of the tourist as for practically everything the tourist depends on the escort. The role of an escort begins as soon as a tourist arrives at his/her destination. It continues all through his/her stay and ends only with the departure. Unlike a guide, an escort may not be free from his/her responsibilities at any hour of the day. This is because in escorted tours the job also involves looking after facilitation aspects like facilitation at the airports, hotels and city tours, etc. In fact, an escort is responsible for everything that the tourist group requires at the destination. Hence, the scope of an escort's terrain, skills and expertise are also very specific and may vary according to the purpose of visit, though at the same time having some common traits while operating a tour. Depending upon the nature of the tour, an escort is supposed to perform the role of an accompanying manager and at times may also has to act as a subject expert. You are already aware of the duties and responsibilities of an escort . Besides facilitation at the airport the tourist may be escorted to a:

- specific place of his/her interest,
- rural areas,
- specific geographical region,
- historical sites,
- shopping centres,
- metropolitan area, and
- business sites, etc.

As an escort when you have to manage a tour knowledge of tourist's expectation would always be an added advantage in charting out your course of action. In fact, to manage your tour effectively you must do an exercise on profiling of the tourists even before their arrival. This profiling is done primarily for creating and developing an awareness and understanding of the tourist habits and attitudes. This exercise in advance helps you in customer care and also to provide quality services. Besides, tourists demand from their escorts' accuracy and authenticity with regard to the knowledge of facts, astuteness, to deal with tricky situation and sympathy with regard to their own problems. The escort should, therefore, be particularly thorough with facts, resourceful and full of understanding for the demands and problems of the tourists. On the other hand, as a manager in the company you have to ensure that the escorts working with you go for this exercise before the conducting the tour.

Once you have recruited escorts, you have to familiarise them with your company's objectives, rules and regulations, besides a full knowledge of the services that you have promised to the tourist in your package. An escort must also know even things like how to file an FIR at a police station or whom to contact in case of emergencies. You must also remember that the escort provides you crucial feedback about the tourist's experiences and the quality of tour operations and in fact there should be general instructions to him for filing tour reports after every escorted trip. What you require in these reports should also be clearly specified and the best thing is to have proformas made in this regard.

Changes keep happening over as regards rule-regulations, etc. and hence, on the job training, upgradation of knowledge and information are other aspects that require a manager's attention, vis-à-vis, training of quality escorts.

You must remember that an escort is the frontline manager of your company who is in direct contact with the tourist for most of the time and hence, any deficiency in escort services will lead to a bad image of your company. For providing the best, the escort should be a satisfied person which means that the company takes care of the employee in the sense that he is adequately paid and is offered incentives by the company. The tendency to hire cheap escorts with insufficient skills and knowledge should not be encouraged. Even when you hire the services of an escort you must look for trained professionals in the area of operations. There are occasions when under lure of money by others, some escorts may try to divert your business by offering them the packages of others for repeat visits etc. You should be very clear while handling such situations and must discontinue the services of such escorts.

Chapter-8

MANAGING TRAVEL AGENCY OPERATIONS – I (Managing Internal Operations, Technology)

Q1. "Managing internal operations in a travel agency requires all managerial skills." Comment.

Ans. It's true that managing internal operations in a travel agency requires all managerial skills. The successful travel agent's series of data desires to be very cosmic and regularly growing. A job description in this regard would include all of the following elements:

- His/her prime responsibility is to negotiate the terms and conditions for commission with principal suppliers. These commissions constitute major source of revenue for any travel agency.
- Recruitment of trained manpower from time to time is yet another important responsibility of a manager in travel agency operations. Right kind of human resources are considered as most valuable assets for any organisation.
- Once the recruitment is over, the orientation/induction programmes shall be arranged by the manager. For existing employees training and development programmes must be arranged in areas which need regular upgradation. For example, technological advancements have forced us to train our employees to work on new technologies or day to day changes in visa regulation, airline/rail schedules, airlines banking settlement plans, etc. require constant upgradation of knowledge. Undoubtedly, training programmes in such areas would not only improve the efficiency of the employees but would also add to the brand name of the company in relation to efficiency and customer care.
- It is also the responsibility of manager to departmentalise the agency for effective functioning and accordingly deployment of required manpower can be done. It is for you to assess that how many people will be required in international section and how

many for domestic section. In other words, it is for you to decide that how many people shall form a part of operations, marketing or any other department for that matter.

- Scheduling of manpower and machines to be made available for the agency operations will also be your responsibility, i.e., how many vehicles you will require for pick ups and transfers or for your staff transportation, how many personal computers to be installed and which one shall be connected with WAN (Wide Area Networking) or LAN (Local Area Networking) to facilitate the transfer of data without loss of time.
- As a manager you need to gather and assess feedback from your suppliers and consumers, which would also help you in designing your products. For example, if your feedback reveals that your customers have more liking for activity packed packages, you shall naturally prepare such packages. Your job doesn't ends here. You must also try to find out what was the level of satisfaction of your customers after consuming your product/services. If some gap is suggested, the consumer must be removed immediately.
- Decision on selection of promotional strategies are another important function to be performed by you. Here you need to address issues like what is the mission of your agency with respect to the image building? What is your target market? How much will be your promotion budget? What would be the most effective means of promotion for your product, most suitable and effective for your target market segment? Above all, how much time you have to build the desired image. For example, many a times situation arises like riots hitting an area, military coup, etc. wherein you have to decide fast on such decision otherwise losses can be irreparable.
- As a manager you shall always believe in sharing information and knowledge with your employees, about competitors, their strengths, weaknesses, corporate business techniques. It is only after this that you can expect them to work more efficiently. You must also subscribe them with various sources of information like trade newsletters, documentary films/CDs, brochures and news bulletins of principal suppliers, current affairs magazines, membership of trade associations, familiarisation trips as well as travel advisories.
- You must train your employees to maintain proper storing and updating mechanism in the organisation. In a travel agency you make most of the bookings on phone and when your customer is on phone line you have very less time to refer to his/her history in your files.

- For effective and efficient operations of a travel agency you need adequate infrastructure. You must ensure that you have provided your staff with equipments like telephones, fax, electronic mails, photocopier and computers in right number and at right time so that they can bear out their functions professionally.

Q2. Discuss the role of technology in tour operations.

Ans. The travel industry of today wears a different look. It is automated and high tech and as a manager it is your prime responsibility to assure the availability of required infrastructure and support systems for the adaptation of technological advancements to manage your business profitably. The list of equipments available for use by your staff may include:

- Telephones,
- Fax,
- Electronic mail,
- Photocopiers, and
- Computers, etc.

These are essential communication equipments in a travel agency which are required for:

- Requesting information,
- Receiving information,
- Making reservations,
- Confirmations, and
- Transmitting information to clients.

Proper use of communication technology saves time, reduces costs and thus, contributes to the profitability of the agency. Having trained staff for operating them and regular maintenance of the equipment are other managerial tasks meant for you. Not only this but the staff should be trained for maintaining records on computers.

The newly emerging computer systems concept of information management can prove to be very useful in delivering accuracy, timeliness, objectivity and relevance to your decisions. More importantly, however, it will lead to the amplification and acceleration of a phenomenon that we have already begun to experience – "creation of a comparative business advantage through information". In fact, the MIS in your organisation should be developed through the latest technological advances.

To achieve desired goals both in terms of customer satisfaction and generating profits for your company you should think of connecting various decision centres at various levels, formal and informal, as an information network with the wide use of computers. You must also acknowledge that the managers/supervisors working at different levels in tourism operations require different types of information to take decisions at right time. Hence, you will need an MIS catering to the management/leadership styles, i.e., if there could be greater user involvement at all stages of MIS lifecycle (MIS lifecycle is discussed at length in MTM-4) then the end results would tend to be superior. As a result the MIS developed by you would help each executive in his/her decision making process while identifying the problems, generating and evaluating the alternative course of actions as well as to acquire necessary feedback on implementing his or her decision and if the requirement arises to take corrective actions. Other important area where technology can be applied is in purchasing or procuring procedures so that malpractices can be overcome as is given in Figure.

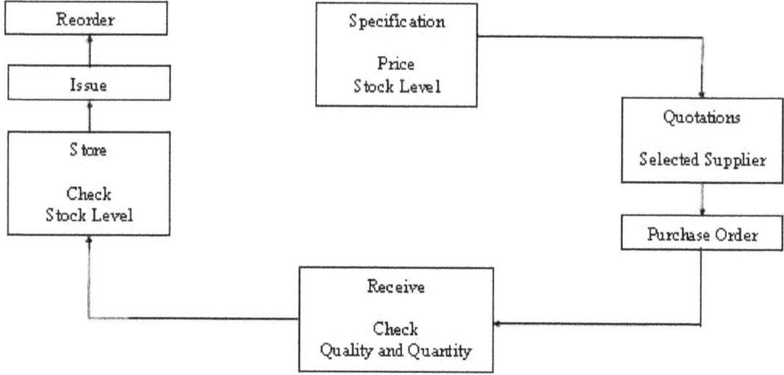

Inventory records can also be maintained with the help of computers. An example of such a worksheet prepared on computer is shown in Figure.

Sl. No.	Stock Description	Opening Balance	Quantity Received	Date	Quantity Issued	Date	Balance	Stock Level to be maintained	Record Quantity
1)	Letter Heads	1,000	2,000	15.3.96	2,500	30.5.96	500	2,000	
2)	Ticket Wallets	1,000	5,000	20.3.96	3,500	1.6.96	2,500	2,500	
3)									
4)									
5)									

However, it must also be noted that the basic management concepts of planning, organising, directing and controlling are essential in travel agency business and should be suitably carried out with the usage of technology as per the requirements. Besides, the role of technology can also be witnessed in the tasks of planning itineraries, ticketing, reservations, dealing with principal suppliers, marketing and sales or deciding on further expansion, the management concepts are of much use in providing guidelines to make best use of available resources.

Q3. Discuss the inhouse operations in tourism organization.

Ans. For soft operation of the agency, departments have been shaped for domestic and international travelers. Both the sections are placed under the charge of efficient managers.

Domestic Departments: Besides ticketing, travel agency also provides hotel and transport booking service to their diversified clientele. Against the receipt of payments from clients necessary vouchers are issued to them.

These service agents are paid commissions varying from 9% to 20% depending upon type and volume of business. These commissions form the major portion of agents' revenue generation.

International Department: You are familiar that International department deals with preparation and promotion of tour packages both inbound and outbound. Most of the tour operators prefer to use services of travel agencies to reach the desired target market segment. Thus, it becomes imperative for you to establish coordination with travel agents. In other words, you are not only required to keep track of various promotional activities undertaken by tour operators but also you need to judge the selling aptitude and potential of the employees of the travel agency because your commission largely depends upon the volume of business generated by your agents. You are also advised to maintain close links with tour operators to know about various promotional schemes and incentives being offered by them or by their principal suppliers. For example, selling a package to Australia can get your clients free two days accommodation at Malaysia or Singapore or Bangkok as an incentive.

It is important to remember that deal is not successful until and unless the client returns from his/her tour satisfied. For this very reason, it is advisable for you to keep in touch with your client and smoothen various transactions taking place at the place of visit. Information about travel documents and other precautions like medical, etc. should be conveyed to the client and any special request of the client should be conveyed to the tour-operator. It is important to point out here the concept of delegation of power can be achieved by teaching your subordinates about the work process. A good service to any client, old or new will ensure a lifetime relationship with them.

Similar mind set should be maintained while dealing with tour operators. Keep in touch with them to ensure a pleasant and successful deal for both your client and the tour operator. A good professional and personal relationship with your tour operator will ensure that even in the time of high demand low supply periods, your principle supplier will help you out.

As in the case of ticketing, do keep a record of your tour bookings. Record should tell you at one glance about the name of the tour operator and tour, tour price, commissions, clients' name, address, profits and so on. Try to maintain a record of after sale and tour feedback report from your client because it will help you in telling your principle suppliers about the areas where they lack client insight. It will also help you to know both your client and tour operator better. One way of ensuring that your first time client becomes life time client is by making them feel special, say by the way of word of welcome or thanks for your visit by the manager.

Q4. What are the sources of revenue.

Ans. Any entrepreneur would expect his/her manager to generate as much as revenue possible for the company and travel trade is not an exception to this golden principle of setting up any business enterprises. Thus, it becomes imperative for you to understand various traditional and modern avenues for revenue generation in order to satisfy the very basic reason for your existence in the trade. The sources of revenue can be classified in the following manner:

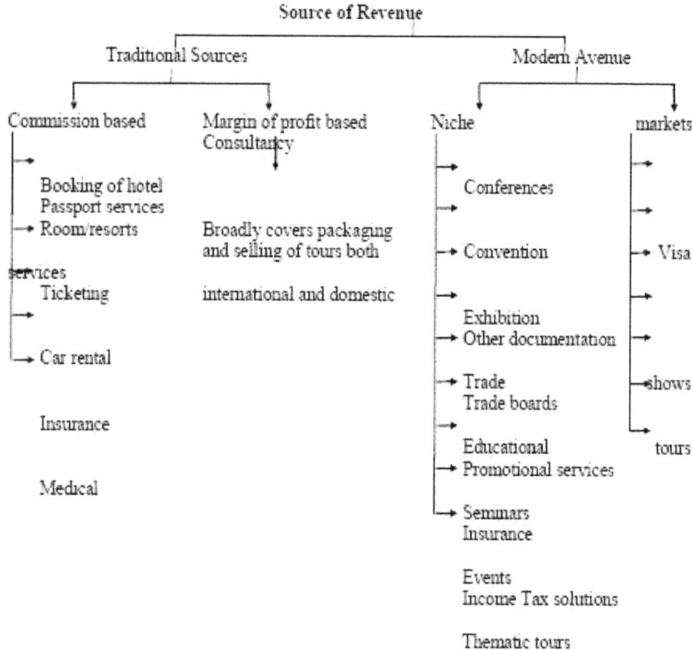

From the above given illustrations it becomes clear that the traditional sources and commission based services in the area of accommodation, airline ticketing, rail ticketing, car rentals, insurance services or even overseas mediclaim covers can generate only the commissions fixed as per the trade norms. For example, if on a hotel booking you may get as much as 20%, on an airline seat you can only manage to get 9% to 10%. However, on car rental rate of commission can be as high as 30 to 35%. On domestic ticket commission rates vary from 4.5% to 5% in comparison to commission on rail ticket booking of just 0.5% to 1%.

Traditionally and even today, travel agents largely depend upon these commission earned from the sale of these services. Therefore, as a manager you must make it a point to generate as much as sale possible for these services so that even when revenue from other services start declining during off-season, revenue from commission keep coming in your chest. Here it is important to underline one fact that rate of commission offered by principal would vary according to volume of business generated by you. For instance, if you are giving booking of 500 rooms to a hotel in one season it is obvious that this particular hotel will offer you higher rate of commission in comparison to a hotel who is given less bookings by you in a season. Same principle applies to other services also which are being sold by you in return of commission. Many a times rate of commissions also depends upon other factors and not merely upon volume, e.g., your negotiations with the principal suppliers, your physical location, your financial credibility, your previous performance record and so on. All these factors centres around your performance as manager.

On the other hand, margin of profit-based services provide you complete freedom to package and sell services both as specific and tailor-made up as profit margin. More and more travel agents are moving in to the area of designing and packaging services since it renders better opportunities for revenue generation. Here we can take up an example of a resort located at a remote place, offering rooms at 40% of the rack price to you. You in return package it and promote it through your brochures at rack rate offering 20% discount to your sub-agent or partners of Global Distribution Networks (GDN). In the end if we see selling such products prove to be more profitable than commission based products/ services. Today you can negotiate with airlines or hotels for bulk booking as consolidators and retail these services with your mark up to meet your administrative expenses incurred as well as to earn reasonable profit margin.

Besides, the traditional sources of revenue, i.e., commission based and profit margin based as discussed above, agencies have explored number of other areas which can substantiate their revenue generation during lean period. These avenues may also be termed as niche areas like meetings, incentive travels, conferences, exhibitions and expositions (MICE); educational tours, event managers, thematic tours as well as special interest tours. In each of the abovementioned category your job would be to identify market segment with such special requirements, assess their specific requirements and supply the same with expected level of satisfaction. In other words, if you succeeded in planning, organising and managing these niche areas efficiently, they would prove to be rich in revenue generation as compared to other components of travel trade operation. MICE is one niche area which is catching the attention of all travel agencies because it has proved its potential as a strong source of revenue generation all over the world. However, you must remember on thing that when you are handling any event belonging to MICE you are expected to render a basket of services, i.e., ticketing, hotel, transport, meeting planning, sightseeing, secretarial services and other business related services to your client as desired by them from time to time.

Devoted to this fact can bring repeat and referral business from a lot of corporate clients. You must, therefore, attach greater importance to the recruitment of best people available in the job market.

In the post jet age, when hundreds of millions of people have started crossing international boundaries, this has created the vacuum for travel agencies to play the role of travel consultants too. In other words, more and more people are approaching travel agents for passports, visa endorsements or for other documentation facilitation services which otherwise prove to be quite time consuming for them. Consultancy charges for such service vary from case to case and from agency to agency. But the established fact is that the revenue coming from these services also contributes significantly to total earnings of an agency. Another upcoming trend in travel trade is to become a representative board of a particular tourist destination or for a set of hot tourist destinations. In other words, you assume the responsibility of marketing and selling these destinations in your country. The understanding aspect of this source is that if negotiated well, you become the sole distributor of services in that destination. As a result of these practices, destinations like Sri Lanka, Australia, Singapore, Seychelles and Switzerland have gained grounds in India and as in consequent outbound tourism from India to these countries has gone up drastically. For example, Thailand is marketed and packaged so well in India by trade board representatives that our outbound tourism has gone up to a figure of 2,00,000 tourists a year against only 20,000 tourists coming to India from Thailand. Fortunately, Indian tourism season is very well defined as a result revenue flows in evenly if well managed by you.

In short, we can say that ample opportunities exist in travel trade for revenue generation. You need to identify and harness these opportunities. If you are able to identify any new area, you would be able to reap higher revenue in the initial stages. Therefore, you are advised to look out for new avenues, either at your own or in collaborative manner with destinations or their principal suppliers so as to achieve not only maximum revenue yield but also to gain a brand image of an established agency.

Chapter-9

MANAGING TRAVEL AGENCY OPERATIONS – II (Dealing with Principal Suppliers)

Q1. How does a travel agency deal with principal suppliers?

Ans. A travel agency is a retail business, that sells travel related products and services to customers, on behalf of suppliers, such as airlines, car rentals, cruise lines, hotels, railways, sightseeing tours and package holidays that combine several products. In addition to dealing with ordinary tourists, most travel agencies have a separate department devoted to making travel arrangements for business travelers and some travel agencies specialize in commercial and business travel only. There are also travel agencies that serve as general sales agents for foreign travel companies, allowing them to have offices in countries other than where their headquarters are located.

Today many small service providers are connected with the modern tourism industry. These small vendors have to face lot of pressures because of the changing business environment.

The environment of the market is so much competitive. The involvement of the technology in the process makes the changes. The customers have the choice to select the best service as well as product for their use. The relationship of the agency from the main supplier is in the process over many years. The companies mainly appoint the travel agents and the agency to sell their product in front of the customer and to make the customer familiar with their product. But now, the concept is changed, the travel agents are working as the consultant as well as management companies for the tour. They show that their main aim is the customer. Some days ago we saw only companies have the major share in supply of the services but now we also found much competition in this field also. The travel agency providing the best packages to the customer and the price of the package is also competitive. The agencies are choosing the best supplier for their product. The changes in the environment also give change in the policy and the strategy of the companies. The agencies are looking that kind of supplier which can be able to give the best quality and service to their customer. In the past, the agencies choose that type of supplier which can give them the best commission. It is true that if we give them the best commission. It is true that if we cannot be able to give the best quality of service to our customer we can't run so long. So, it is very important that we should give the priority to the quality not to the profit. The travel agencies are giving much priority to the range, quality, type and price. Without the proper management we cannot achieve the goal. So we can achieve these things by:

- By giving them all the facility at single outlet.
- Minimize the processing time.
- Management the information by the help of technology.
- Saving through the effective administration.

Every principal supplier mainly work to achieve the goal by minimize the cost of its functions and increase the market share by the help of effective distribution channel. Travel agency helps the management to achieve all kinds of aim by selling their products and packages in front of the customer.

It is very important than supplier as well as the agency will work hard to achieve the main aim. Without a proper and long-term agreement between two, no one can be able to achieve the main goal. The main suppliers can be different according to their nature of service but the tour operator helps them in selling under a package. It is the responsibility of the tour operator that he should work hard to provide each and every part of their service to the customer. We should measure the things that the service promise by the main supplier is matching with the main service or not. We should make these things in a proper manner by:

- Many times the tourist faces the problem of health care at the tour. So, the main supplier should provide them a quality of health service or they should have a good insurance company with them to deal with this kind of situation.
- Surprise checking of the principal suppler service. We should check his ability, his punctuality with time, and quality of the service. It is very important to check the past experience of the principal supplier on the basis of the safety provided to the customer.
- It is very important that we should take a kind of approach which can help us to achieve the aim without any problem. The main supplier helps us in each and every task of the tour. Some time the agencies prefer the supplier on the basis of their commission and incentives. But without quality we cannot be able to achieve the profit and growth. So, for that we should make all the things clear to the main supplier.
- Sometime the risk of safety is very high for the tourist. So, it is our responsibility that we should make the things in a manner in which the risk should be less. If we are not going to provide the

safety and the security to the tourist that can create a big problem for us

Q2. Highlight the challenges being faced by the players of tourism industry while developing and sustaining relationships.

Ans. From the origin of this industry travel agents have enjoyed healthy relationship with tour operators. This relationship is based on the mutual benefit for both the trade partners. If tour operators want to sell their products/services they ne ed retailers and the travel agents fill this gap by acting as their intermediary. However, today this relationship is facing natural challenges from the market conditions, i.e., travel agents are forced to act as tour operator to sustain themselves in the trade. As a result, there exist thread line difference between their function and huge gap in their relationship. In the recent times tour operators have started reaching to their customers directly due to cut throat competition and price war. You must have seen in the newspapers even big tour operators have started advertising their special tour packages designed for all sections of the society be it up market or budget market.

The travel agent component of the tourism industry is a prime example of an industry that has undergone immense environmental changes. For example, the most contributing supplier airlines has seen significant macro-economic changes which are often volatile, i.e., rising, then dropping and recently rapidly rising jet fuel prices have its reflections on the costs of tickets. Similarly, the periods of recession and economic growth, demographic changes and deregulation of the airline industry have all affected relationship within the tourism industry.

In a survey conducted by National Bus iness Travel Association (NBTA), U.S., over 350 corporate travel professionals, 56% cited reduction in travel costs and 45% said improved security procedures at transportation gateways, can turn around business travel volumes, trimming travel costs and strengthening buyer/supplier relationships are priorities for most respondents. 67% said they have increased contact with preferred partners in past 12 months and 53% have seen corporation implement cost-cutting measures. According to the survey most of the travel managers have reached out to suppliers, with 78% saying that they have sought and renegotiated current contracts and 75% said that they have increased contracts with alternative suppliers. On the other hand, according to the same survey, suppliers are implementing more alternatives to normal booking channels in order to reduce their distribution costs because 86% of suppliers say that there have been increased sales as companies have now being seeking alternative travel suppliers with lower costs. (Website: NBTA) If we look at the whole gambit of relationship between agent and principal supplier from this changing perspective we see that competition has intensified in the travel market place, forcing down margins. Airlines have cut commissions and accelerated the availability of net fares in the hope of driving down their distribution costs.

For agents, the handling of principal suppliers has also become difficult due to the forces of globalisation which are transforming the way our corporate customers conduct their business, i.e., through internet as a perfect medium for the sale of distributed products with instantaneous delivery.

This change is sweeping all through our industry and there can be no going back. Airlines aren't going to remove the caps or raise commission to the levels of the past. The internet is here to stay. Booking and ticketing processes will get more and more automated.

With the rise of the web and the development of call centres airlines have the chance to take back, direct control of their passengers. This has reinforced new phenomena, i.e., internet travel agents such as e-bookers or expedia. In part this is because airlines are under pressure to sell a product with a limited lifespan. A seat on an aeroplane is worthless when it is empty to take off. Therefore, challenge

is to sell these unsold seats before takeoff. In response to this demand online bookers have online auction of unsold seats at last minutes. For example, if a cross-Atlantic unsold seat is auctioned at US$ 50, it is betting on net loss because even after meeting travel agents' commission, payment and fee, global distribution system fee and ticketing charges, airline itself is lucky to see 50% of total amount, i.e., US$ 25. Thus, airlines as a princip al supplier shall admit that they cannot survive alone.

Even when these airlines reduce commission, travel agents would manage to compliment their efforts with wafer thin margins. It is also because of the fact that travel agents and payment card companies know more about an airline's customers than it does. From this point there can be two-way movement, i.e., either some big players in different sectors could form partnership to break up airlines. For example, partnership between an online travel agency and AOL/Time Warner could create a virtual airline, hiring jets, crews, maintenance facilities and any other necessary services to undercut real world airlines who are their partners other movement can be that airlines join hands with banks and other organisations in providing products and services for defined target markets. Everybody will benefit. The single action of buying an airline ticket from the partnership website will trigger a chain of cost saving and cross selling opportunities. For instance, airline will immediately save ticket commission of upto 15% plus charges for distribution, ticketing and reconciliation. The bank on the other hand gets payment card fee and if one of its smart card is used the ticket details themselves can be downloaded directly on the chip, eliminating ticket printing and distribution costs. This would pose a challenge for travel agents to gear up and upgrade their websites. Though airlines have websites specifically designed for them, but it would be intermediaries who should make the running travel agents shall make airlines realise that more is ordered through

them, lower would be the operating cost for airlines and moreover airlines can do away with the inherent fear of sharing information which otherwise has become diff icult for them.

Another important challenge before the intermediaries of present times and future would be to develop two sets of business relationships, i.e., one relationship with customers and one relationship with suppliers. You should build one set of relationship primarily around the needs of your customers because without them you have no business. You should be able to analyse what are their needs and to

what extent you are able to deliver them. Business travel is projected to be growing at a faster rate than holiday tourism; therefore, you are advised to carefully analyse the needs of corporate customers.

These corporate customers have primarily three priorities:

- They want their execution to be well cared for,
- They want to see costs come down, and
- They want to put more effective travel management operations in place.

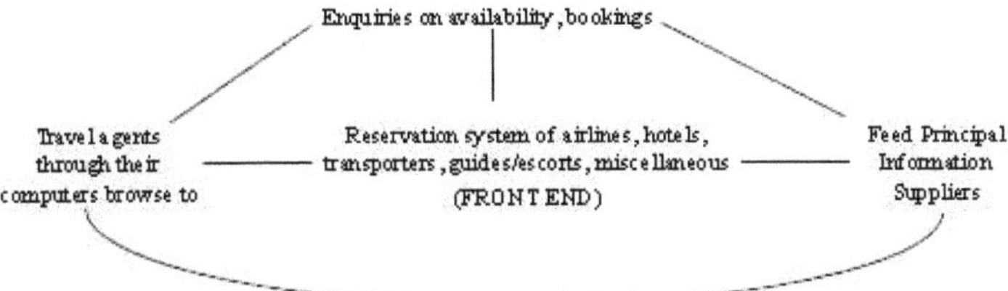

All these priorities of corporate customers can be met by creating a healthy and competitive environment by you.

As far as relationship with suppliers is concerned it is advisable to develop front-end business descriptions.

This is effectively a value added service to enable the distribution of leisure travel and tourism products between principals, tour operators and travel agents. It enables to maintain 'many-to-many' "trading relationships". This "many-to-many" trading relationship can be illustrated as:

Figure clearly illustrates that the front end gets you a generic (but customisable) user interface allowing you the entry of booking details with enhanced navigat ion and information facilities. This kind of front-end user, if used by you can render following benefits:

- It gives you ability to make multiple, simultaneous enquiries for a holiday using only one set of data entry stream;

- It enables you to have effective link between front and back office system and thus gaining improvement in managing customers and providing customer service;
- You can speed up your booking process by taking full advantage of high network speed of this front-end intranet facility;
- It allows you automatic search on preferred supplies system, i.e., matching your commercial needs with that of supplier in line with existing business practices;
- When you are handling higher value sales in your presentation it enables you to make images and video clips;
- When you are using this facility cost of sale is known to both principal as well as tour operator;
- It generates detailed and accurate management statistics regarding booking transactions;
- Because of the use of the interface platform principal and travel agent are able to give better support to the retailers in the form of customer specific sales and marketing information as well as customer service; and
- Its use allows both principals and tour operators to maintain their market penetration whilst enjoying the benefits of the technological change.

To sum up, we are witnessing a rapidly changing scene in travel distributions driven by technology advances and an increasingly competitive market place. We are facing new issues and challenges more particularly related to the use of intranet and internet facilities which need to be carefully addressed for developing a healthy relationship between principals on one hand and tour operators and retailers on the other hand. In modern marketing terms it can be called business-to-business (B2B). E-commerce is becoming increasingly important topic to be addressed in the marketplace. The major challenge before you would be to survive in the age of e-commerce which is largely being used by suppliers as their distributors' network. For instance, when they introduced tickets to eliminate the paper tickets that customers were accustomed to, having delivered to them by agents. In short, time has come where principal suppliers would do everything possible to bypass the travel agents to avoid paying commission and to recapture principals relationship with their customers.

Q3. What kinds of challenges are presented in the promotion of the tourism industry in India?

Ans. As per the Travel and Tourism Competitiveness Report 2009 by the World Economic Forum, India is ranked 11th in the Asia Pacific region and 62nd overall, moving up three places on the list of the world's attractive destinations. It is ranked the 14th best tourist destination for its natural resources and 24th for its cultural resources, with many World Heritage sites, both natural and cultural, rich fauna, and strong creative industries in the country. India also bagged 37th rank for its air transport network. The India travel and tourism industry ranked 5th in the long-term (10-year) growth and is expected to be the second largest employer in the world by 2019.

According to the Travel & Tourism Competitiveness Report 2009 brought out by the World Economic Forum, the contribution of travel and tourism to gross domestic product (GDP) is expected to be at US$ 187.3 billion by 2019.

But still there are some challenges and problems that Indian tourism industry has to face in present scenario.

After the 11th September Attack in the Asia region we come to know that the growth of the industry is also affected. The negative impacts come on the growth of the industry. What kind of opportunities can watch in the Indian tourism industry are:

- Antique civilisation
- National destinations
- Culture
- Wide rage of traditions
- Different religious places
- Festivals
- Mixture of urban and rural area

It is very essential for the Indian industry t hat we should work hard to make the people aware about our destinations. If we are not able to make the people to know about the Indian places, than it should be difficult for us to make the people to come India. It is essential for the country like India that her tourism industries should work hard to develop that kind of infrastructure and the culture by which they can give the competition to the develop countries in tourism. But the main challenges are present in the Indian tourism industry:

- India has the poor infrastructure in comparison to other countries.
- The conflict also in between each and every area of the country to getting high number of tourists.
- According to the tourist the facilities present in India are not able to give the competition to the facilities present in the other countries.
- India is facing the problem of security for the tourist. From past few years the incidents against the tourists affect the image of the country in the world.
- The tourist thinks that the public transport as well as the condition of the transport in India is very bad because you require a high amount of time to reach any location.

- Tourist think that the environment in India is very unhealthy for them by which they can easily affected with any kind of germs or the diseases.
- Indian government as well as the organisation does not provide the proper information to the tourist to reach to one to another place.

In the present situation the ITDC has developed many kind of things to promote the Indian tourism industry in the world but it is very much required that they should develop and do the things time to time to promote the Indian tourism industry like:

- It is essential that ITDC should provide the adequate facilities to the tourist and develop the good environment give the healthy information to them.
- It is very much require that you should develop the present modes of transport present in the country. In the cities like Delhi it is very difficult to reach within the time.
- The government should provide the adequate fund and the facilities to their state organisations to develop the tourism in the state level.
- Tourism information should be providing the each and every location and it is better to update it time to time. We should make a king of system by which the tourists are easily able to access each and every information within the time.
- It is required that the government should solve the problem by which the tourist who come from outside India not feared about their security.
- Make the visa facility easily available to every one by which more and more tourists will come to India.
- Give permission to the private sector organisation by which they can promote the tourism in a large scale.
- Design the package according to the requirement of the tourist and make changes according to their requirement.
- Make some promotional plan by which we can easily promote our destinations in the other country.

In India there is large opportunities are present for the tourism industry. It is very much required that the organisations which are dealing in the tourism industry should work to promote the industry on the world platform because it attacks the earnings of a common man of India.

Q4. HOw we deal with Air Travel Provider.

Ans. Among the varied range of travel services, air carriers assume greater importance as principal suppliers. Mode of travel, time and cost related to it affect the decision making of the tourist consumer and is applicable in case of both – domestic as well as international air travel.

(1) Domestic Air Travel: Sales of domestic air travel is made through airlines and travel agents. In domestic air travel market elements to be considered are:

- All players offer almost parallel services and aim to create strategic competitive advantages through the development of software application and customer loyalty programmes like Frequent Flyer Programme (FFP),
- In marketing terms, airlines have two priorities, the retention and growth of market share and distribution cost reduction. As you have already been told that market share of any airline largely depends upon its distribution network. Distribution cost reduction obviously increases the competitiveness and profitability of the airlines,
- The channels of distribution network receives commissions from the airlines for the services provided. The rate of commissions paid are negotiated and agreed upon in agreement between the airlines and agent. Thus, one agent may receive more commission from one airline than the other,
- Increasingly airlines and travel agents are using information technology to improve their competitive position. As a result, for agents the handling of their principal supplier has also become difficult due to the forces of globalisation which are transforming the way our corporate customers conduct their business, i.e., through internet, as a perfect medium for the sale of distributed products with instantaneous delivery. As we all know this has already swept all through this industry and there will be no going back. Airlines aren't going to review the cap or raise commission to the levels of the past. The internet is here to stay. Booking and ticketing processes will get more and more automated, and
- Now you can handle your supplier by asking for following practices: (a) point of sales discounts; (b) discount for different types of payments, e.g., direct debiting, EFT or credit cards, etc.; (c) special discounts for using preferred carrier on individual bookings; (d) rebates for achieving a percentage usage of a particular (preferred) carrier; (e) discounts for group bookings; (f) discounts for travellers travelling in off-season; and (g) percentage discount on certain non-trunk international routes.

On the other hand, when you are booking for your customers, you must convince your customers that if earlier the bookings are made better would be the discounts available, higher the discount greater would be the number of conditions while negotiating with airlines. Thus, your objective shall be to make your buyers overall cost of travel attractive rather than just offering good discounts.

While handling your airline as supplier it would be advisable to base abovementioned discounts on the lowest logical fare. In practice you must know that there can be only three exceptions from taking lowest logical fares;

- when application of discount on another fare is cheaper;
- when discounted full economy fare which offer flexibility achieve a comparable cost; and
- where the overall costs of a fare and associated management cost is comparable when you are purchasing a higher cost fare.

As you know that the fees for service arrangements, an agent is employed by the customer rather than by the airlines, thus, you charge from the customer the net cost plus an additional fee for the services provided. It, therefore, changes the process from payment of travel agent by the airline to payment of the travel agent by the customer. When you pass this payment to airline on or before the settlement date commission is passed on to you, and you in return, if agreed, pass on partial commission to your customer.

(2) International Air Travel: As you have learnt in your previous Units that the international air travel market is an open market with the diverse and flexible fare structures. International airlines have alliances which are reflected in special fare offers, code sharing and incentive schemes like Frequent Flyer Programme (FFP). Besides a wide range of fares, international air traveller from a variety of itineraries, accommodation type and other services. On the other hand, these choices give option to air traveller as regards what to choose from but on the other hand, these add complexity to the booking of tickets.

You must know as travel agent that international air travel and its suppliers are governed by following elements:

- Since there are many suppliers in the International market and supply and demand have a great influence on pricing when during off season prices go down demand increases, and during holidays even when holidays are sold at premium demand remain unchanged;
- Airlines which aligns their operations often compete in the international market a group by offering special deals;
- Consolidators buy airline tickets in bulk and then wholesale to agents, holiday groups, etc. This can naturally influence the availability of tickets especially during holiday seasons.
- International air travel market is more influenced by changes in fuel price or fluctuation in currency value than domestic air travel market.

Having learnt these elements involved in international air travel you can handle air service suppliers by following practices like:

- since there can be a number of different fares and conditions offered for the same itinerary for overseas travel. Fares for international travel are market driven and can see changes daily, different conditions or numbers of stopovers may apply. Thus, as a travel agent you should obtain the best option for your client;

- If certain international routes are travelled frequently, you should ask for special route fares from the carrier; and
- Discounts and rebates discussed in the case of domestic air travel an also be negotiated in case of international air travel.

Q5. How we deal with Tourist Transport Suppliers.

Ans. When you talk about principal suppliers for tourist transport products you broadly think about:

(1) Private Taxi and Airport Shuttle Operators: When an independent tourist or group arrives in our country, as a travel agent your first job is to arrange the transfer of the same. In other words, you need the services of private taxi or airport shuttle operators in countries like Singapore, Malaysia and Thailand. In our own region, tourists are issued pre-paid vouchers by overseas operators to use airport shuttle services. Hence, you have to maintain linkages with these frontline service providers.

In our country we have constraints of parking space for these private taxis or airport shuttle operators. At one point of time you will find only one or two airport coaches in the waiting area or for pre-paid/ registered taxis at airport are only five to seven hundred. If we analyse the whole situation we find that most of the international flights land at midnight or in the early morning hours, if one flight carries approximately 550 passengers and there are a minimum of 15 flights a day, number of passengers seeking services of these taxi operators or airport shuttle operators would be around 8250. For this number, 500-700 taxis are grossly insufficient. Thus, it becomes all the more important for you to handle your transport supplier in such a manner so that whenever you need their services you can easily find them.

(2) Private Bus Line Operators: This segment of suppliers assumes importance when you are dealing with overseas groups, i.e., when in one season you are sure of booking for 15-20 groups each consisting of 50-70 passengers you would always require the services of these private bus line operators since you will have to move your groups from one tourist centre to another. For example, most of the foreign tourists want to have golden triangle of Delhi-Agra-Jaipur on their itinerary this circuit is normally covered by road. Thus, to have smooth operations of groups you shall have good linkages with them. Sometimes you do not handle your groups rather yo u assign it to some other person located at different place, thus, you shall establish healthy linkages with these private tour operators so that they give priority to your assignments and take total care of your groups.

(3) Operators of Mass Transit Systems: Mass Transit Systems are advanced public transport systems that provide information on availability, location and scheduling of public transportation services and it also facilitate ride sharing. Objective for introducing such system would be to enhance customer service in general, service reliability schedule information accuracy and on time performance while reducing costs in particular. It is believed that more accessible more complete information about transit schedules routes and fares would attract more consumers. When you are in travel agency operation business, you shall ensure that you have been establishing linkages with right kind of operators of Mass Transit System so that you are able to provide satisfactory services to your customers. This will also enable you to provide customer care with regard to provision of information to the customers. Travellers need information concerning schedules, routes and fares before they leave known territory so that they can plan their trips in unknown territory(ies). They may also require your assistance during the course of their trip due to unprecedented conditions or circumstances. These days to provide information at all times and at all places tour operators have either established linkages or have setup their own call centres to answer the inquiries of valuable customers.

(4) Independent Operators of Commercial Vehicle: Independent operators of commercial vehicles can also be viewed as important suppliers for tour operation business. They are also known as independent commercial vehicle operators. These independent operators have a few of the Indian and imported vehicles catering the needs of selected segments of tourism industry. Therefore, it is advisable to be in good books with these operators. To achieve it, you are advised to make their payments regularly, give their staff members training at your own expenses from time to time to introduce your products/packages with the single objective of providing satisfaction and value for money to your customer. These fleet operators play a crucial role in successful operation of your business. These independent commercial vehicle owners are different from **commercial fleet operators** in the sense that latter have a big fleet of vehicles consisting of different sizes and qualities, i.e., both Indian and imported. Moreover, you don't have to provide training to them. They always recruit trained personnel for example commercial fleet operators utilize automatic tracking of vehicles, despatching of vehicles and weigh-in-motion system to improve the safety, efficiency and convenience of commercial vehicle operators. They also subscribe to way-finding and traffic status system (most advanced road signalling systems).

(5) State Government Transport Undertaking: Even today tourists prefer to visit many states of India by road. For instance, Rajasthan, Himachal Pradesh, West Bengal, Maharashtra, Karnataka, Tamil Nadu, are a few areas to name from the list. Attractions in these states, though remotely located, are enjoyed by vis itors due to their accessibility by road or by rail. Wherever tourist be located if he or she has to go to Shimla will first reach to Chandigarh or Kalka and from there proceed to Shimla. Hence, road transport provided by state transport undertaking also plays as important role as airlines or private taxis. It wouldn't be an exaggeration to say that 70 – 75% of about 230 millions domestic tourists use state transport system for their visits. So, it becomes unavoidable for you to establish good linkages with them to get bulk bookings (groups) even during peak seasons.

Feedback is the breakfast of Champions.

Ken Blanchard

You can Help other students.
" Inform any error or mistake in this book."

We and Universe
will reward you for Your Kind act.

Email at : feedback@gullybaba.com
or
WhatsApp on 9350849407

Chapter-10

MANAGING TRAVEL AGENCY OPERATIONS – III (Publicity and Promotions)

Q1. How does a travel agency manage publicity and promotions?

Or

Discuss the packaging and promotion in tours.

Ans. Promotional campaign is needed to bring into the light the tourism industry and tourists about that location. The same holds true for all the travel related services; let it be a cruise, a hotel room or a tour package. One cannot buy something one is not aware of. There is a need for promotional campaign in all the spheres of travel industry to make a tourist or a corporate client aware of the options and choices open to him/ her.

Promotion is mainly used, as a short-term incentive to stimulate the sales of services and normally what is offered through promotions is something extra than what is normally offered in the product or service without charging anything extra. It is a fundamental component in services marketing and it should not be baffled with selling, advertising and publishing. There can be a number of objectives for a travel agency to go for sales promotion and the strategy opted in this regard would depend on the type of objective one has decided upon. For example, if the objective is to retain the old customer you can come out with a discount offer for using your services for the second time. Similarly, if the objective is to counter competitors you may offer something extra than what is being offered by your competitor. In fact many a times it is often a mix of objectives that the organisations tend to set up for promotional purposes. However, you must remember that the objective thus set off should be in compliance with the marketing objectives of the organisation. You must remember the following:

- There is cut throat competition today in this business and hence, innovative strategies have to be worked out to have an edge in the market.

- As a member that what you will adopt and offer will be soon duplicated by others.
- You have to keep a close watch on what extra the others are offering.
- In tourism business there is always the opportunity for joint promotions – explore the feasibility in this regard. You also have the option for simultaneously adopting multiple schemes but don't crowd the options as it may confuse the consumer.
- Your business is affected by many external factors that are beyond your control. For example, if a country has put up a travel advisory to its citizens for not to travel to a particular destinations. It will be foolish to indulge in promotional activity there. On the contrary, this being a political decision, you will have to lobby with your own government to intervene and get the advisory reversed.
- Seasonality is a prime factor in tourism. Hence, time your promotions accordingly.
- Try to develop a brand image for your organisation so that consumer sensitivities in relation to price and expectation etc. have the least impact on your sales.
- External promotion campaigns should be backed up with internal promotion campaigns like giving, incentives bonus or commissions, etc. to your own sales personnel.
- You should not only monitor but also measure the performance of your promotional campaigns and also look for follow up actions.

Besides the above aspects, you have to also ensure the following:

- Be absolutely clear about your target audience.
- You have a complete plan for promotion.
- You have sufficient budget, etc.

Another aspect that is generally not taken account of is caring for the cultural sensitivities not just of your target audience but the society as a whole where the promotions are to be carried out. This is equally true in the case of advertising. In complex societies, even a small slip can attract both social as well as religious protests. We have often seen this happ ening in the case of multinationals that have been insensitive to local customs and traditions. Take for example, the following promotions:

"Come with your girlfriend, buy two cold drinks and share the third – a free drink from us"

Now such promotion may yield good result in a metro but would bring strong reactions in small towns or in a rural society. The same can be the situation in relation to using cultural signs for promotions. For this reason, you should be tremendously alert in this regard.

Q2. Why publicity and promotions are needed in travel agency business? Answer with examples.

Ans. A sales promotion is any type of reduced pricing or bonus deal offered to customers to encourage them to make a purchase. Sales promotions exist in every different type of sales, and may be something as simple as a reduced price at the grocery store or a low interest rate on an auto loan. An advertised sales promotion can be a great way to get customers to come into a business and end up spending additional money.

The promotion campaign is so much important in the tourism business. There is very tough competition in the market by the help of the promotion the company can make an important image in the mind of the customer. By the help of the promotional campaign we give something extra to our customer and make him aware about our product or service. It is very important that we should make some changes in our promotional campaign time to time because the marketer are always ready to copy the innovative ideas of others. So, in the promotions we should require a kind of innovativeness by which the customers automatically attract towards our service and the product. The promotions make us different from the competitors. It is very much important that we should make ourselves aware about the promotional campaigns of our competitors.

The promotion campaigns help us in making the brand image in the market. The promotion campaigns helps in creating awareness and make the tourist to come out from their homes and visit to the place that attracts them. The promotion mix is the effort by which the organisation creates and arouses the interest in the mind of the customer. The promotion campaign not only makes the customer aware about our name but also make them to use our service and the product. It is a tool by which the companies can retain their customer for the long time by giving them a high amount of benefit on the basis of their usage. The promotion campaign should be design in a way by which they can catch the attention of the customer. It is very important that we should use a king of strategies and the policies by which the customer's attention turned in to the desire. In the promotion campaigns the customer finds something special for him.

When we are going for the promotion campaign it is very much require that we should clearly know about our target market? It means we should start the campaign according to the area. The effort should be making in a manner by which we can able to achieve our target and the goal. When the customer doesn't know about our service and the product it is very much required that we can create awareness in the mind of the customer? The promotion campaign helps the company to provide the knowledge of their service and the product in the mind of the customer. The promotional campaign helps the company to make or develop the linking with the customer. By the help of the proper promotional campaign we develop the preference in the mind of the customer. The promotional campaigns are direct mode of communication with the customer by which the customer can-solve his query directly with the seller. So, the promotion campaigns are need for the success in the market for the companies.

Q3. Write the types of Marketing Communication for promotion.

Ans. A variety of media are used to execute a promotional campaign. One must take the services of an expert in this field in order to select the medium of communication. Today, electronic media is surpassing all other mediums but still the print media remains effective too. Generally, advertising on electronic media is backed by advertisements in the newspapers, magazines and journals, etc. Further, brochures, travel videos and travel documentaries have their own role though gradually promotional CD-ROMs have come up in a big way.

For advertising you have to pay but publicity comes free of cost. It is necessary that you have good public relations in both print as well as electronic media so that they can report your promotional activities.

In tourism promotional activities are targeted at intermediaries also as bulk of the business comes through the distribution channels. Some such activities are:

(1) Familiarisation, or FAM, trips. As you know suppliers offer FAM trips to travel agents and tour operators and travel writers so that they can experience a product firsthand. These FAM tours are usually offered free or at minimum cost. They are used by airlines (to promote new routes, new destinations, and new aircraft), by hotels (to promote new properties), and by government tourist offices (to promote cities, regions or whole countries as tourist destinations). The theory behind the FAM trip is that "you cannot sell what you haven't seen".

(2) Sales contests. These are sponsored by suppliers to reward travel agents who sell a certain number of airline tickets, hotel rooms, cruises, and so on. These points can be utilised by the agents, operators or can also be encashed by them. When they are encashed some part of this is transferred to the clients.

(3) Travel trade shows, travel marts and travel seminars. Held for members of the trade, these gatherings offer an excellent opportunity for government tourist offices and suppliers to meet face-to-face with travel agents and other distributors. They are particularly effective forums for promoting new products and services.

Promotional Activities: In some cases sales promotional activities are one-time events used to stimulate consumer packaging. They may be targeted at prospective clients (to encourage them to buy the product promoted) or at travel agents and tour operators (to motivate them to sell the product). Sales promotion directed at the consumer includes:

- Special offers, such as promotional airfares and hotel rates, free gifts with purchase, and free trips offered as prizes in contests. Travel fairs and exhibitions. These are particularly effective promotional events, because they allow suppliers to reach a large number of potential travellers in a single location. Sales literature is distributed at the event.
- Travel nights. These are staged by travel agencies and sometimes co-sponsored by suppliers. Travel nights are often used to promote tours and cruises. Wherein prizes may be awarded to further stimulate consumer interest.

Q4. Write an essay on Public Relation.

Ans. Public relations, or PR, the third of the main promotional techniques, is used to reinforce advertising and sales support activities. It can be defined as the use of planned communications efforts to create a positive image for a company and its products. Unlike the other forms of promotion, it is not directed at prospective clients or travel intermediaries, but rather at journalists, editors, travel writers, and other media representatives. Travel companies target these individuals because they are in a position to create and influence public opinion.

Typical public relations activities include press releases, press conferences, guest appearances on radio and television, and FAM trips for travel writers.

A press release, the mot commonly used PR tool, is prepared by a travel agency or tour operator and mailed out to newspapers, magazines, and television and radio stations. The release might announce an inaugural flight; all a new package the opening of a hotel, travel agency, or government tourist office; the introduction of a new product or service; or a visit of VIP to your hotel, e.g., when Bill Clinton visited India and preferred to stay in a Sheraton group hotel gained force of cost publicity. It may also include any other newsworthy event.

A press conference is used to publicise travel-related events. Instead of sending out a press release, the company holding the press conference sends out invitations to reporters from the print and broadcast media. Those attending the press conference are issued a press kit with background information on the company and its new product or servic e. If the press conference achieves its goal, the event will receive favourable coverage in the news media.

Guest appearances on radio and television talk shows give travel company representatives an excellent opportunity to promote their products at no cost. All expense-paid FAM trips for travel writers can be a very effective way to receive publicity. They can backfire, of course, especially if things go wrong (maybe a missed flight connection or a bad choice of hotel). Public relations has much in common with advertising in that it aims to promote a product, a service, or a destination. There are, however, important differences between the two:

- Public relations involve the securing of free media space or time. No payment is made for the print or broadcast of press releases. For this reason, public relations is sometimes referred to as "free advertising".
- Because it is written or printed by a third party, public relations tend to have more credibility than advertising. People are often sceptical of the advertising message, but they are inclined to believe what they see, hear, or read in the media.
- On the negative side, promoters have far less control over public

relations than advertising. A press release, for example, may be edited or not even used to all. In addition, public relations is hard to evaluate because of the difficulty in measuring its cost effectiveness.

In tourism word to mouth publicity plays a vital role in promoting a destination or a service. For example, as a tourist before booking your air tickets you do ask your friends which airlines they travelled, how was the service and many tourists come to a travel agency predetermined on the airlines they will travel or the hotel they would like to stay. You must have trained staff to handle such clients and in case you want to sell some other airline or hotel your staff must be extremely cautious not to loose or annoy the customer.

Chapter-11

MANAGING HOSPITALITY OPERATIONS: ORGANISED SECTOR

Q1. Discuss the hotel classification system in India. Enlist various requirements to be fulfilled for the classification.

Ans. Hotels in India are amongst the most visible and important aspects of a country's infrastructure. Indian Hotel industry is closely linked to the Indian tourism industry. India being the most sought-after tourist destination of world which is regarded as travelers' paradise offered snow-peaked mountains, heritage sights, beautiful landscape, exotic wildlife, palm-fringed beaches, historic monuments, Ayurvedic treatment and many more. With increasing globalization, Indian hotel is catering to the tourists around the world with all the facilities required for making the tourism sector a success. This country of Maharajas is home to the world class hotels ranging from Palace Hotels, Deluxe/Luxury Hotels, Heritage Hotels and Five Star Hotels to Business Hotels, Economy Hotels and Cheap Hotels. You have to just name it and India has it! Here brief information is given for various types of hotels.

We can classify hotels on the basis of infra-structure, facilities and services that are provided by them. Broadly speaking hotels can be classified on the following basis:

- room charges or price, i.e., budget, luxury, etc.
- range of facilities, i.e., five star, no star, etc.
- location, i.e., resort, etc.
- length of stay, i.e., transit, residential, etc.
- ownership and management, i.e., chain, individual, etc.

Types of Hotels

- **International Hotel or Star Hotel:** These hotels are modern western style hotels located in almost all metropolitan and other large cities as well as at principal tourist destinations. Usually, they are located at a prime location in the city.

  These hotels are luxury hotels and are classified based on an internationally accepted system of classification grading. There categories range from 7 to 1 star grade depending upon the facilities and services provided by these hotels. In addition to accommodation various other facilities are provided to make the stay more comfortable. These facilities include – information counters, banquet halls, conference facilities, a number of shops, travel agency, desk business centre facilities, money changing and safe deposit facilities, theme restaurants, beverages, swimming pool, gymnasium, health clubs and other entertainment programmes in the form of games, music and dance, etc.

Price of the room varies depending on the category of hotel. The facilities available also affect the pricing. Usually the clientele is business executives and up budget tourists. It is important to note here that the categorisation of hotels into stars is not mandatory in some countries but it delivers some satisfaction to guests that he/she is using a graded hotel.

- **Non-Star or Commercial Hotels:** At every tourist destination one comes across hotels which do not come into any classified criteria. These hotels mainly depend upon individual travellers, middle budget tourists and many of the guests are repeat guests. These hotels are located near the business or commercial centres of the city and have easy access to transportation. They provide accommodation, parking space for guests and their visitors, restaurants and sometimes business centre facilities as well.

  Size of such a hotel varies from small to medium. The rooms of these hotels are priced lower than International hotels.
- **Residential Hotels:** These hotels can be described as an apartment house complete with hotel services. They are also referred to as apartment hotels. These hotels are largely located in big cities and they mostly operate under the European Plans where no meals are provided to the guests. Though in United States, room service along with maid and valet services are provided to the wealthy guests in the luxurious residential hotels.

  The concept of residential hotels started in America where people found that permanent living in hotel offers many advantages. These are very popular in United States and Europe.
- **Floating Hotels:** As the name suggests, these hotels are located on the surface of the water. It may be on seawater or river water or even on a lake. These hotels provide all the facilities and services of a hotel and are very popular with the tourists. In many cases, across the world old ships have been converted into these types of hotels and have become popular among the tourists.

  The size and price depend upon the hotels. Sometimes they are part of a hotel chain or they can be owned by individuals as in case of the houseboats in Kashmir.

- **Capsule Hotels:** Capsule hotel is the latest innovation in the budget hotel market. The first of its kind was opened in Osaka, Japan in the year 1979. Now, they have mushroomed not only in big cities of Japan but also in other parts of the world.
  The capsule is a box made of glass reinforced plastic or cement, open either at one side or one end in which they provide some functions of a traditional hotel such as a bed, a clock, radio, colour TV, flexible lighting, a box for valuables and a miniature table for writing. Rooms in a capsule hotel are lined up in a double decker fashion along with a central aisle as in a sleeping compartment of a train.
  Toilets and washrooms, vending machines and lounge area are clos e by on each floor of the hotel. The function of each capsule is monitored by a central computer system and security is controlled by close circuit TV cameras. They mainly cater to the business travellers. The low tariff and vintage locations are the major factors for their popularity.
- **Transit Transient Hotels:** As the name suggests their location are in close proximity of the airports, catering to guests who stay for a limited period of time from few hours to a few days. This category may include any type of hotel providing temporary accommodation to its guests.
- **Heritage Hotels:** Old properties of the royal and aristocratic families are renovated and the old aura is recreated for the tourists to stay in heritage surroundings. The heritage properties are an attraction in themselves and the best example would be the state of Rajasthan and Gujarat in India, which have made huge profits by using the concept of heritage.
  Paradors in Spain and Posadas in Portugal are castles and other historic buildings that have been converted into hotels by the government. They cater primarily to vacationers, offer full meal plans and are reasonably priced. More luxurious castle accommodations are available in France (Choteaux) and in Germany and Austria (Schlosse). These heritage properties render a valuable and memorable experience to their guests when they serve them as nobles or members of royal family.

Motels: The basic difference between hotel and motel is that it provides parking space to the travellers travelling by automobiles and the rooms opens to the parking lot. The history of motels can be traced back to tourist cabins which were located near highway, catering to businessmen travelling by road.

Tourist cabins gave way to Tourist Courts which provided the same services and facilities but it became a 24 hours business. They offered 20 to 24 rooms around a central parking space with some garage and refuelling facilities.

The concept of motels became very popular in America as the automobile travelling increased. Over the time many motels started adding a lot of extra amenities such as swimming pool, restaurants, business centre and in-room television became standard features. And thus, these motels also started attracting vacationers as well.

Resorts: A resort hotel is one which is visited by holiday maker or tourists for relaxation, recreation and/or for entertainment.

Resort hotels cater to tourists and are located near place of some scenic beauty, i.e., the sea, mountains or in 'off the beaten track destinat ion'. These days, resorts are also found in wildlife sanctuaries or national parks.

The primary reason, as is mentioned earlier, for visiting a resort is rest and relaxation and these hotels are built with the objective of indoor recreation activities giving visitors special welcome and atmosphere of informality.

The services and amenities offered by resorts include swimming pool, tennis court, skiing, boating, surfing and many others. The clientele of resort hotels is mostly persons with considerable income looking for relaxation and recreation.

Resorts can be of various types and can be classified on the basis of climate and topography. Broadly, they fall in the following categories:

- Summer Resorts,
- Winter Resorts,
- All Seasons Resorts,
- Hill Resorts, and
- Health Resorts.

A majority of the resorts are seasonal establishments and provide special facilities and other concessions to the guests with a view to extend their seasons of operations.

Time Share Apartments/Condominiums: Concept of timeshare, is also popular as vacation ownership or holiday ownership, offers the purchaser the right to enjoy, for a set period or interval, each year, vacation time in an apartment or other type of lodging that is a part of a tourist complex, equipped with a variety of services and facilities. In other words, it is effectively the advance purchase of time in holiday accommodation.

The period of time sold is usually based on modules of a week, fortnight or a month. Across the world people enjoy the value of timeshare. Timeshare concept grew into a major phenomenon and large number of people started using it only in 1980s and 90s. Origin of this concept can be traced back to 1960s. Since then it has become a global product. Consumers have option of more than 4000 timeshare resort projects being consumed by nearly 3.1 million purchasers worldwide. This impressive growth is largely due to value of this product and its market appeal which doesn't recognise any geographical boundary, age or social status. Above all, it provides flexibility and variety to the holiday experience and choice for purchasers to choose from world's most exciting holiday destinations at a very reasonable price.

It is believed that more attention will be placed on recreation and personal renewal, on cultural and educational stimulation, and on a sense of balance of life that not only purchasers will simply leisure but also need in its basic sense. Why and how this will happen. To answer this question we can refer to report of a recent US survey of more than 2000 timeshare owners entitled – "Timeshare Ownership Benefits", conducted by Ragataz Association, following results were recorded:

- 82% believe that timeshare has had a positive impact on their vacation planning;
- 73% enjoy vacations more as timeshare owners;
- 70% agree timeshare has allowed them to stay in higher quality accommodation;
- 68% have developed a greater sense of confidence that they can travel and vacation without worries as a result of owning timeshare; and
- 65% find they have more opportunity to spend quality family time together during vacation.

The growth of timeshare at an annual rate is of over 15%. Since the 1980s it can be compared with that of travel and tourism overall (4%) and hotel accommodation (2%) in the same period. However, timeshare in the context of world tourism is still a relatively insignificant part and can be seen from the following broad comparison:

Estimate of Timeshare Related Tourism as Percentage of Total Related

Timeshare owning households worldwide (m)	Average family size	No. of intervals owned per family	Estimated nos. of timeshare related trips (m)	Total no. of vacation trips inc. domestic	Time share related as % total
3.14	3.6	1.5'	17	5,000	0.35

Q2. Explain the role of safety and security in organized accommodation sector.

Ans. In these troubled times, safety and security should be one of your main concerns.

The guest always wants the survey of their security and safety. Most of the guest chooses a type of hotel where the security is up to the mark. The security should require a proper concentration from the management.

It is very essential that we should develop the safety standards by which we can able to deal with any kind of emergency problem. If we neglect the safety concern, that can become a big problem for us in future. If the things wants some repairing than we should work for them within the time. The safety of the guest should be first priority of the hotel. The hotel makes a proper department who check all the concern of the safety daily.

The security is always a point of matter in the hotel industry. The hotel should work to develop a high class security in their hotel. The hotels have the guest all over the world, so the people always want a high standard of security near the hotel premises. The problem of terrorism is become the main issue in these days. The terrorist attack on the Taj Hotel is also motivating the hotels to develop a full proof security. The security also checks the things that the activities of one guest should not create a problem for another guest. Most of the hotel gives the contract of security to the private agencies but some develop their own security department and adopt the retired people from the army. The security department should make a proper policy to deal with any kind of emergency situation. The security staff should train of deal with any kind of emergency situation in the area.

Q3. What are the various forms of hotel ownerships?

Ans. Hotel policies primarily decide the direction for the operational aspects of a hotel. Usually, the type of ownership plays an important role in the formulation of the hotel policies. The type of ownership can be:

- **Individual:** This means the owner is completely independent with regard to policy formulation and operating procedures.
- **Chain Ownership:** A chain owns the hotels, formulates policies for them and staffs it with its own employees.
- **Lease and Joint Venture:** An individual or a chain can operate a hotel without owning it by entering into a lease arrangement. Here a fixed monthly rent is given to the landlord or a profit sharing is agreed upon.

  In joint ventures, two companies or two individuals or a company and an individual form a partnership and start a hotel with profit sharing policy.
- **Franchisee:** Under a franchise scheme, a hotel owner contracts with an established chain to operate the property under the chain name. The owner of the hotel or franchisee pays an initial development fee and a monthly licence or franchise fee.
- **Management Contracts:** Under a management contract one company owns the property and another (the chain) operates it.

The principles and policies of the hotel are thus formulated keeping in mind the type of ownership of the hotel. According to **S. Medlik**,

- A customer policy normally says what the hotel is aiming to do in terms of its markets and quality standards of what it provides, includes its concept of good value and its approach to price, discounts and credit; it states its attitude to complaints and refunds.
- An employment or personnel policy covers such matters as recruitment, selection and training; remuneration, conditions of

employment, welfare; promotion, retirement, termination; consultation, negotiation and the handling of disputes.

- A shareholder policy defines what the owners are entitled to expect in terms of their rewards, information and participation in the business and what is expected from them.
- A policy towards supplies postulates what is expected from them regarding the quality of supplies, delivery and terms, and how each can expect to be treated by the hotel. On the second level policies dealing with the guidelines of discharging functional responsibilities of the hotel like financial management, marketing and sales and purchasing are decided

On the third level, policies relating to the hotel product like food and beverages and accommodation are decided. Usually a few policies are set and guidelines are decided in relation to them. These are forwarded to the respective departments so that departmental operational policies can be formulated.

Once the policies are formulated, it is necessary to get them written down and be communicated to all the concerned departments and personnel. The hotel policies can be viewed as the objective of the hotel. But to attain these objectives certain plans needs to be followed strategies are these plans.

According to Michael Olsen, an organisation's strategy can be formulated in variety of ways:

- **Environmental analysis:** an assessment of the organisation's specific competitive environment, as well as the activities taking place in the more general environment affecting all businesses in an industry. The purpose of this process is to identify the threats and opportunities that present themselves to the organisation over the planning horizon under consideration.
- **Analysis of the organisation's strengths and weaknesses:** a thorough analysis of the internal resources (such as human, capital and material) of the organisation for the purpose of determining what the organisation does well and what problems it needs to address.
- **Strategic gap analysis:** a review of the organisation's strengths and weaknesses in the context of the threats and opportunities presented by the general and task environment.
- **Mission statement development:** the preparation of a statement defining what is the present position of the organisation and where it intends to reach? The mission statement identifies the target audience for which the organisation will provide goods and services and clarifies how these will be provided and the standards by which they will be judged. This statement is the result of the

analysis of the organisation's environment, its strengths and weaknesses, and the strategic gap.

- **Strategic alternatives analysis:** the identification of the types of possible strategies that can be used to achieve the mission of the organisation.
- **Evaluation and selection of strategy:** a thorough evaluation of the possible strategies available to the organisation and the selection of the one(s) that will best fit its needs.
- **Monitoring and follow-up:** the establishment of expectations and standards to control the process of strategy implementation and to determine the effectiveness of the chosen strategy.

A lot many classification schemes on strategic management are there but only a few are appropriate in regard to the hospitality industry. One such classification is by Schaffer who postulates the following strategy types:

- **Do-it-all differentiators:** attempts to build an excellent reputation within the industry; attempts to be an innovator in service processes; continuously look for new market opportunities; and seeks high quality of services.
- **Internalised resource conserver:** strives to develop and refine existing products and services, aims to procure as much as possible in the raw material state.
- **Narrow focussed marketing innovator:** has a narrow product focus, engages in environmental scanning activities.
- **Efficiency/quality controller:** relies upon experienced and trained personnel to provide quality service.
- **Geographic focussed price leader:** seeks stability in operating environments, develops conservative capital structure policy; interested in price leadership, serves only specific geographic markets.

Similarly, West and Olsen's definition of strategy types can also be used in regard to hospitality industry. It consists of the following categories:

- **Innovation and development:** places major emphasis on innovation in menu design; develops new products and services; serving a specialised market and emphasising efficiency.
- **Focus:** emphasises services to a specialised market; strongly oriented towards efficiency and differentiation.
- **Image management:** emphasises the use of advertising and innovative marketing promotions to achieve market share.
- **No strategy:** seeks to be everything to everybody with no strong orientation towards any area.
- **Differentiation:** emphasises the offering of a unique product or service to a specialised market that is insensitive to price, strongly oriented towards the control of operations and market area.

- **Control:** attempts to exert strong control over operations; an internally oriented organisation.

According to **M. Olsen** the four major components of the implementation process are:

- Successfully performing the recurring administrative tasks associated with strategy implementation.
- Creating a fit between the organisation's internal processes and the requirements of a strategy.
- Making adjustments for the organisation's overall situation in which implementation must take place.
- Choosing how to lead the implementation task.

It is important to note here that to implement a strategy, the organisation must have in place systems designed to match the resources of the organisation with the chosen strategy. Also leadership is an important ingredient in the successful implementation of the strategy.

Q4. Enlist major benefits of operational budget.

Ans. Financial management describes the process through which a firm makes financial decisions within the framework of the firm's goals by interpreting and analysing financial data. Financial management is a functional responsibility which is required to discharge other functions of the hotel. Without financial management operational functions cannot take place.

It is primarily with concerned with two aspects – raising funds and managing funds within the organisation with the help of budgetary control.

Funds or capital refers to all of the company's liabilities and owners' equity, including short term and long-term capital, preferred stock, common stock and retained earnings. Short-term debts refer to all debts due within a year. Long-term capital debts are funds payable beyond one year. Bonds are another widely known form of long-term debts. The other type of long-term capital is equity funds provided by investors who are interested in owning a portion of the business. Once funds are raised they are allocated by budget.

Types of Budget: According to Raymond S. Schmidgall, budgets can be classified as:

- **Capital Budget:** The focus is on the acquis ition of property and equipment. The capital budget includes the list of property and equipment to be obtained over the next several years.
- **Cash Budget:** Its focus is to monitor cash flows. Cash budget simply reflects expected cash receipts and cash disbursements for a period of time.
- **Operational Budget:** It reflects forecasted revenues and expected

expenses for the hospitality business for a period of time. When an organisation "exceeds the budget", it is almost always the operational budget. The targeted profit is reflected in the operations budget; thus operations budget gets a lot of attention.

According to R.S. Schmidgall, major benefits of an operations budget are:

- The budget provides a clearly understood plan for management to follow. It includes targeted prices to be charged, labour rates and expected hours, amounts to be spent on marketing and so on. The plan can be easily followed by managers, even those who join the hospitality enterprise in the middle of the year, when it is reduced to writing and clearly communicated.
- The budget process requires that managers be involved with its preparation in order to consider alternative courses of action. They must answer a multitude of questions, such as What prices should be charged? What services should be provided? What level of quality of these services should be provided? When the operations budget is adopted, management has decided on what it believes is the best of the many alternative plans.
- Budgeting requires management to examine just what measures are required to generate the desired results – most often a net profit. Certainly managers are dealing with the unknown since the budget pertains to the future; however, they are faced with keeping projected expenses lower than forecasted sales.
- Budgeting provides a standard of comparison, i.e., the budget is the basis for comparing the actual results of the accounting period. Any major differences should be carefully analysed to determine the cause and appropriate action taken to correct the problem.
- Budgeting allows management to look forward and prepare for the future. For example, if new equipment is required for a new menu item, then the equipment should be obtained in plenty of time to have it functioning properly when needed.
- When participative budgeting is used, i.e., when those managers who are to be held responsible are involved in the budget process, then these managers feel they have ownership of their budgets and as a result they will be more motivated to expend energy to achieve their plans. Budgeted numbers forced on managers quite often results in managers blaming the budget preparers for poor budgeting rather than accepting responsibility.
- Finally, the budget process provides a channel of communication whereby the firm's objectives in numbers are communicated to all management levels. Further, as time passes the actual results are compared to the budget, both of which are furnished periodically to managers who are responsible for the actual results.

The following stages would be useful while preparing a budget for the hotel:

- **Establishing Financial Objectives** wherein the board of directors of the hospitality organisation decide upon the firm's financial objectives.
- **Forecasting Revenue** wherein revenue generating operation such as rooms and food and beverage department's revenue is forecasted based on past records and future plans.
- **Estimating Expenses** wherein the expense to be incurred by the various department like food and beverages as well as marketing and others are estimated.
- **Determining Net Income** where the expected net income for the year is determined.
- **Reviewing and Approving the Budget**, it is now that the whole executive reviews the budgets and then forwards it to board of directors for approval.

Once the budget is approved, operational budgetary control methods need to be followed for proper financial management by each department.

Q5. Draw and describe Typical Organisation Chart for the Marketing Effort of a Large Convention Hotel.

Ans. To run a hospitality organisation successfully, effective marketing of the product is necessary. Marketing management is defined as the planning, organising, leading and controlling of marketing activities. An understanding of the hospitality marketing mix is necessary for the successful marketing management.

Marketing theorists in the hospitality industry have attempted to modify the way in which the marketing mix is viewed in order to make it more specific for the hospitality marketer. **Renaghan** (1981) suggested that the hospitality marketing mix is made up of three sub-mixes:

- the product services mix, which is defined as a combination of products (tangibles) and services (intangibles);
- the presentation mix, which includes all of those activities that a firm uses "to increase the tangibility of the product-service mix in the perception of the target market at the right place and time"; and
- the communications mix, which is basically the totalit y of communications between the firm and its target market.

To these three sub-mixes, Lewis and Chambers (1989) added the distribution mix, which they define as "all channels available between the firm and the target market that increase the probability of getting the customer to the product". This definition of distribution is different than the definition for tangible products. In marketing tangible products we are concerned with getting the product to the customers in their own homes. For most hospitalit y products we are more concerned with how to get customers to the hotel or restaurant so that they can consume our services.

Here comes the marketing department of the hotel. A typical organisation chart for the marketing effort of a large convention hotel is given in Figure below.

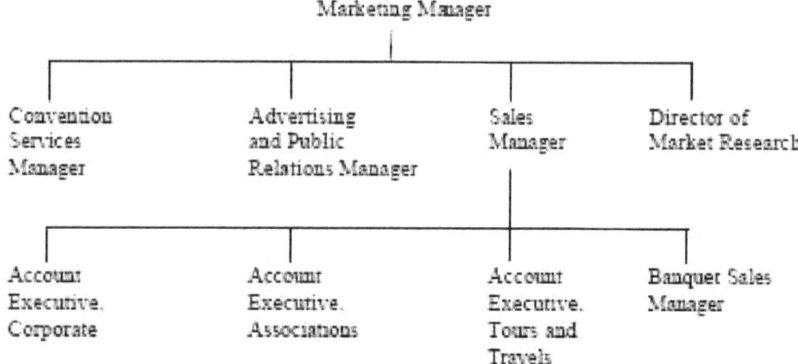

The job for the marketing department becomes a little tough since here the production and consumption of product takes place simultaneously. Also the intangibility factor of the product creates unique problems. Therefore, before using the marketing mix – market research and selection of target market is necessary. Only then marketing mix comes into action.

First, Hospitality Product Mix is decided where good and services are both integral part of the servic es. So F and B means both the food as well as the services of the people concerned. Hospitality Communication Mix or promotion consists of all the activities a hospitality firm uses to reach its target consumers. At least three books list a wide variety of techniques available for hospitality industry communications. Hospitality Pricing Mix depends on the demand as the room rate for a similar kind of room at different location vary as there is a lack of demand. Second is competition which can be either indirect as the various options available to the traveller or direct, i.e., from the various hotels of similar standard vying for the same target market. Third is the cost.

- The inherent fixed costs associated with "being" in business, i.e., those costs that remain the same regardless of business volume (depreciation, administrative salaries and so forth).
- The variable costs associated with "doing" business, i.e., those costs that vary with business volume (materials, direct labour and so forth).

The market positioning is, in other words, customer perception. The rate would be too high or low to customer depending upon how they perceive the product. The menu pricing, however, take various other methods of sett ing menu prices.

Finally, Hospitality Distribution Mix entails the use of various channels of distribution. The marketing department has to ascertain which channel to use.

Chapter-12

MANAGING FRONT OFFICE OPERATIONS

Q1. The efficiency in front office operations has a lasting impact on customers. Comment.

Ans. The Front Office function of a Hotel is to act as the public face of the hotel, primarily by greeting hotel patrons and checking in guests.

It also provides assistance to guests during their stay, completes their accommodation, food and beverage, accounts and receives payment from guests.

Department is typically composed of Reception, Reservation, Concierge, PBX (phone service system), Telephone etc.

The number of interactions and transactions between the guest and the hotel during a guest

stay, determine the type and nature of front office operations. The stages of guest stay are:

- pre-arrival,
- arrival,
- occupancy, and
- departure.

Various trans actions between the guest and the hotel, therefore, depend upon the stage of the guest stay. The transactions can be best understood by going through the guest cycle.

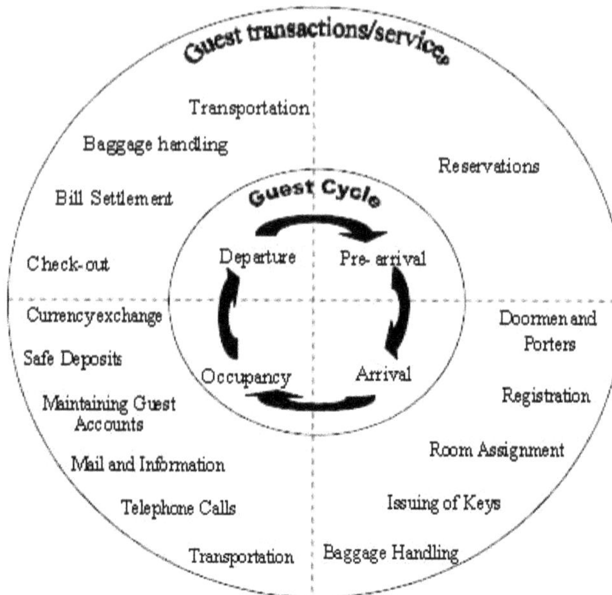

Figure above shows the following transactions and exchange of services between a guest and the hotel:

- reservations,
- check-in and registration,
- mail and information,
- uniformed service and baggage handling,
- telephone calls and messages,
- handling guest accounts, and
- check-out and bill settlement.

All these services and transactions are handled by the front office department. The functions and services of the front office department can be differentiated depending upon the area where they are being performed. Some of the functions are performed by the reception desk as front-of-the-house operations and rest are performed as back-of-the-house operations. Table below gives a brief summary of the functions performed by the front office as described by Michael I. Kasavana.

FUNCTIONS	AREA OF OPERATIONS
1) **Sell guest rooms** Accept reservations Handle walk-ins Perform the registration process	Front of the house activity
2) **Provide information on hotel services** Concerning internal hotel operations About external events and locations	Front of the house activity
3) **Coordinate guest services** Liaison between front and back-of-the-house areas Handle guest problems and complaints	Front of the house activity
4) **Chart room status reports** Coordinate room sales and housekeeping: occupied status On-change status, out-of-order status	Back of the house activity
5) **Maintaining guest accounts** Construction of folio and account Posting to folios (updating) Supervision of credit levels Documentation of guest's transactions	Back of the house activity
6) **Settlement of guest accounts** Preparation of guest statement Reconciliation of folio Perform the checkout procedure	Front of the house activity
7) **Construct guest history file** Record the guest's personal data for future references	Back of the house activity

Front office is the centre of the activities related to the hotel. The operations which occur in the front of the guest are called front of the guest are called front of the house operations. These operations are done through the interaction with the guest. When the guest makes any call for reservation then these kinds of operations start. Firstly information is gathered related to the guest and the verification of the reservation is done. Front of the house operation means the direct interaction of us with the guest. The front of the house operations is very much responsible in making an image in the mind of the consumer. If we are able to make an impression, it helps us in future growth.

After complete verification, Guest check in is done which is the common activity for all types of the guest. In check-in process information is needed which will then make the data record. Normally this process is computer based and almost same in various kinds of hotels. The collected information can be utilized in the future and also plays a vital role in strengthening the relation of guest and the hotel. The information also helps us in the emergency situations.

Front of the house operation includes:

- Decision related to sale of room to the guest.
- Availability of the room.
- Maintaining the guest account.
- Providing room services.

Checkout process includes bill making, decisions regarding account settlement. It is also a function of the front office.

Back-of-the House Operations: After checking, the account of the guest is activated. When the room is allocated to the guest, his account status comes to the play? Now every financial transaction made by the guest is recorded financial transaction made by the guest is recorded in his account. Transaction can be in the form of laundry, food items, phone calls or any other service. In the daytime, front office staff is busy in doing the other activities. At night, back of the house comes into the play, all the transactions from the morning to the night is updated to the account of the guest. There scan be a credit limit predetermined by the hotel and the hotel give permission to the guest to make payments before the check-out if he wants. There are two modes of payments, guest either provide their credit cards during check-in or cash at the time of check-out.

Use of property management system is also rewarded the great significance, in this method guest is provided information related to his account daily through the T.V. monitors in their room. By this guest is relaxed at the time of check-out. He does not have to wait for the bill a too long.

Maintenance of the guest record and the data is activity of back of the house. It also maintains the occupied and vacant room status with the housekeeping department. It is very important for the organisation that their front office and the back office work together to gain the mutual benefit.

Q2. Discuss the significance of front office operations in tourism organizations.

Ans. Apart from of the rank or kind of the hotel, front office is the most visible and important focal-point of a hotel.

It plays an important role in providing hospitality to the guests. It is responsible in developing the relationship of the guest and the hotel. The behaviour, communication skills, efficiency of the front office sets the first impression of the hotel. The main part of the front office is the reception desk which is the place where all the front of house activities is conducted. The role of reception desk is to reserve, receive, register, assign rooms to guests, and maintain the accounts etc., and it acts as a regular source of information to the guest during their stay in the hotel.

Its functions are given below:

- **Selling the Room:** It includes accepting the reservations and completing the registration process. The selling of the rooms is the main task which is complete by the front executive. Managing all the front office executive is a task which is done by the senior manager in the company.

- **Delivering Information on Hotel Services:** It is related with the internal hotel operation, external events and locations. The front office executives have all the information related with their functions and the functions of all the employees in the hotel. The front office executives works as a key between all the departments in the organisation. The hotel operations information is also available at the front office.
- **Maintenance of Guest Account:** It creates the account updation, determination of the credit limits and documentation regarding transactions. It is the responsibility of the front office executive that he should take all the relevant information related with the guest. The customer fees and the extra payment registers are also managed by the front office executive.
- **Coordination of Guest Services:** Provide better services and solutions to the guest problems. If the guest is facing any kind of problem it is the responsibility of the front office that they should work to solve the problem of the person in pure and the proper manner. The front office manages all the service related with the guest in the organisation.
- **Settlement of the Accounts:** It prepares the bill and performs the checkout process. The bills management and clearing the all check out procedure is the task of the front office. The welcome task and the good bye task are related with the front office executive.
- **Making the Guest History File:** For the future references, record of guest is maintained. The guest file maintenance is also the task of the front office executive. The management of the data help the organisation to retain their customer.
- **Handling the Correspondence:** Handling all kinds of correspondence is also a task which is handling by the front office executive in a proper manner. The incoming as well as the outgoing correspondence is purely and the properly is managed by the front office executive.

Q3. Briefly describe the process structure in service organization.

Ans. A successful service process design in one condition can be a poor choice in another. A process design that gets customers in and out of a fast-food restaurant quickly would not be the right process design strategy for a five-star restaurant, where customers seek a leisurely dining experience. Further, a good design strategy for the servers at a restaurant might be totally inappropriate for a process back in the restaurant's business office. Economists sometimes put service organisations into different industry classification, such as financial services health services, education, and the like. Such distinctions help in the understanding of Different Dimensions of Customer Contact in Service Processes

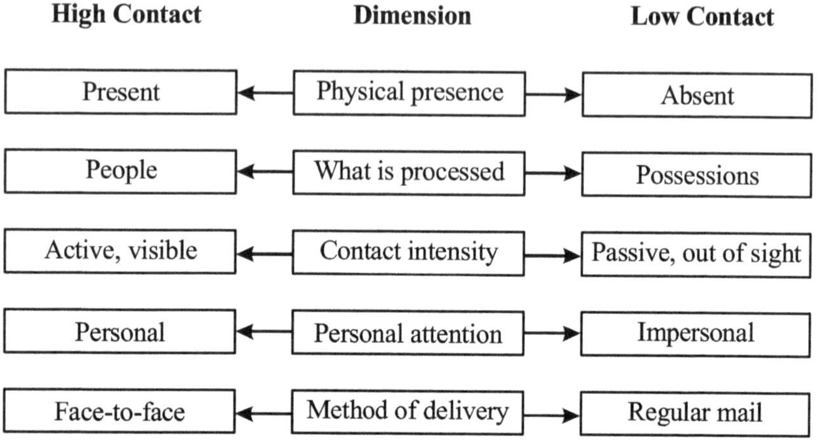

aggregate economic data and perhaps even some general tendencies on process design choices within a firm. However, the classifications are not very helpful when it gets down to designing an individual process. For example, there is no standard blueprint for how work should be done in the banking industry. To get insights, we must start at the process level and recognize key contextual variables associated with the process. Only by starting at the process level can we recognize patterns of appropriate designs and see how decisions should be grouped together.

A good process design for a service process depends first and foremost on the type and amount of customer contact. **Customer contact** is the extent to which the customer is present, is actively involved, and receives personal attention during the service process. in contrast with a manufacturing process, the customer can be very much a part of the process itself. The Figure shows several dimensions of customer contact. The nested-process concept applies to customer contract, because some parts of a process can have low contact and other parts of process can have high contact. Further, even a subprocess can be high on some dimensions and low on others.

Above Figure shows only the two extremes of customer contacts, but they really represent a continuum. Thus, many levels are possible on each of the five dimensions. Only when they are taken together can you truly measure the kind and extent of customer contact. For example, the customer may not be physically present, but may still have high contact by being actively involved in the process, such as with eBay and other forms of Internet interactions that are managed without any face-to-face contact.

The first dimension is whether or not the customer is physically present at the process. Customer contact at a process is important, regardless of whether the customer is internal or external, and regardless of whether the service process is at a manufacturing or service organisation. The amount of contact can be approximated as the percentage of the total time the customer is at the process, relative to the total time to complete the service. The higher the percentage of time that the customer is present, the higher the customer contact. Face-to face interactions, sometimes called a *moment of truth or service encounter,* brings the customer and service providers together. At that time, customer attitudes about the quality of the service provided are shaped. Many processes requiring *physical presence* are found in health care, hospitality services, and passenger transportation. Physical presence also exists at a manufacturer's service processes, such as when a marketing representative (internal customer) receives information for putting together a bid on a customized product. During a face-to-face meeting with an industrial engineer and accountant, they collectively make some key decisions on how the product will be manufactured and priced. When physical presence is required, either the customer comes to the service facility, or the service providers and equipment go to the customer. In the first case the service operations is fixed in place, and in the second case the service provider and equipment are mobile. Either way allows the customer to be preset while the service is being created.

A second dimension is *what is being processed* at the service encounter. *People-processing services* involve tangible actions to customers in person. The service is provided to the person, rather than *for* the person, and so it requires physical presence. Customers become part of the process, making the service's production simultaneous with its consumption. *Possession-processing services* (many such processes are found in e-commerce, freight transportation, equipment installation, maintenance and repair, and warehousing) involve tangible actions to physical objects the provide value to the customer. The object must be present during the processing, but not the customer. The service is consumed after the process is finished, rather than simultaneously with the service's creation. Customer contact is also established with *information-based services,* which collect, manipulate, analyse, and transmit data that has value to the customer. Such processes are common in insurance, news, banking, education, and legal services. Internet processes also fit within this category, where there is no face-to face contact during the execution of the service. The figure does not list contact process, examples of information-processing services exist where the customer is quite active and contact is high without face-to-face contact, as we discover in the next dimension.

The *intensity of customer contact* goes one step beyond physical presence and what is processed. It deals with the extent to which the process accommodates the customer, and it involves considerable interaction and service customization. **Active contact** means that the customer is very much part of the creation of the service and affects the service process itself. The customer can personalize the service to suit her particular needs and even might decide in part how the process is performed. Active contact usually means the process is visible contact. **Passive contact** means that the customer is not involved in tailoring the process to meet special needs or in how the process is performed. Even if the customer is present, he may simply be sitting in a waiting room, standing in line, or perhaps lying in a hospital bed. Many processes where the customer is present but the contact is passive can be found in public transportation or theaters. Interaction with service personnel is limited.

A fourth dimension is the extent of *personal attention* provided. High-contact processes are more intimate, and they exhibit mutual confiding and trust between the service provider customer and the serviced provider. When contact is more personal, the customer often *experiences* the service rather than just receiving it. The customer is changed in some way. Impersonal contact lies at the other end of the customer-contact continuum. At a less intimate process, for example, the customer might move through a standardized work flow or stand in line at a ticket counter.

Customer-Contact Matrix for Processes

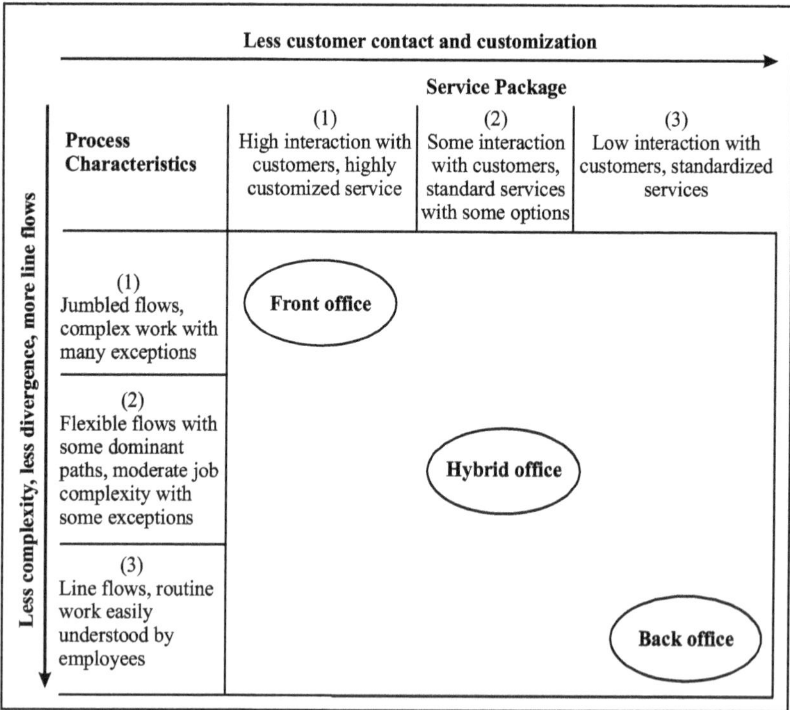

A final dimension of customer contact is the *method used* to be in contact. A high-contact process would use face-to-face or the telephone, assuring more clarity in identifying customer needs and in delivering the service. A low-contact process would likely use a less personable means to deliver the service. Regular mail or standardized e-mail messages would be the preferred way to exchange information for low-contact process. The advent of the Internet and the widening channels of electronic distribution channels allow processes that traditionally had high customer contact to be converted into low-contact processes. Retail banking is a good example, where customers can go to the traditional branch bank or they now can do their banking online.

Q4. Write a short note on front office.

Ans. A front-office process has high customer contact where the service provide interacts directly with the internal or external customer. Because the customization of the service and variety of service options, the process is more complex and many of the steps in it have considerable divergence. Work flows are jumbled, and they very from one customer to the next. More freedom is allowed or inherent in the steps and sequence of the process. There are many exceptions to the usual work pattern. Not only are there more steps in the process, but employees find them more difficult to understand. There is more service variety and services are more customized, at least to the extent of having many standard service modules (as with mass customization). The high-contact service process tends to be adapted or tailored to each customer, and the customer has more choice in how each step of the service process is carried out and sometimes even where the service encounter occurs. An example of a front office, as illustrated in Figure, is the process of the sale of financial services to municipalities. This process is highly customized to meet specific customer needs, with customer contact, complexity, and divergence all quite high. The process flow is jumbled, depending on customer requirements.

Front Office:

Sale of financial services

(1) Research customer finances

(2) Work with customer to understand customer needs

(3) Make customized presentation to customer addressing specific customer needs

(4) Involve specialized staff offering variety of services

(5) Continuing relationship with customer, reaction to changing customer needs.

Chapter-13

MANAGING HOUSE KEEPING OPERATIONS

Q1. Write an essay on housekeeping operations in star hotels.

Ans. When selecting the best hotel for a vacation, most people will assess the size of the rooms, hotel amenities, location and reviews. An important factor that is usually overlooked unless it is unsatisfactory, is the work of the housekeeping staff. These hardworking individuals ensure that messy rooms are miraculously spotless at the end of the day. Hotel housekeeping is a difficult and demanding job that requires much more than might be expected.

Importance of Housekeeping

- Housekeeping is the department that deals essentially with cleanliness and all ancillary service attached to that.

- The standard plays an important role in the reputation of the hotels. One feels comfortable only in the environment which is clean and well ordered, so cleanliness is important for health foremost also for well being.
- Accommodation in hotels tend to be the largest part of the hotel, it is the most revenue generating department, the housekeeping department takes care of all rooms is often largest department in hotels.
- The rooms in hotels are offered as accommodation to travelers/ guest as individual units of bedroom. Some interconnected rooms are also made which will be helpful to the guest and families. Many hotels offer suits to the guest.
- Hotel offer laundry, dry leaning facilities for guest clothes, shoe polishing facilities also.
- Hotel aims to make environment comfortable and offer specialised service to the guest.
- Hotel offer guest the choice of specialty restaurant, coffee shop. The bar also sells liquors which generate the revenue of the hotel. They are available in banqueting, meeting and private party facilities.
- Revenue can be generated from conferencing, meeting, seminar etc.
- These days shopping arcade also found in hotels.
- A health club is a part of facilities of most large hotels especially resort hotels this also include swimming pool and spa facilities.
- Hotels try to make the ambiance as pleasant as possible by nice colour scheme, attractive furnishing and a well kept efficient staff.
- House keeping is the department determine to a large extent whether guests are happy during stay and in turn mankind they return to the hotel.
- The fine accommodation and service are provided to the guest so they are pleased with the hotel. The guest satisfaction is its primary object and the hygiene factor must always be present in the hotel.

In hotels major part of revenue comes from rooms, rooms which is not sold on any night losses revenue forever and reason for poor occupancy can be anything like hygiene factor, cleanliness, lack of modernizing etc. hence main purpose is to improve whole appeal of the room. A guest spend more time alone in his room than any other part of the hotel, so he can check up the cleanliness he wishes to as some of the guest are more health conscious these days.

He may check up dusting, in-depth cleaning and losses confidence if properly not done e.g. If drawers are not cleaned he may generally won't feel like putting his clothes down. Decent room supplies are service like quick laundry and dry cleaning service shows guest that hotel is considering his comfort and wishes to please him. not only this from the cleanliness of lobby, public area, restaurant, cloakrooms, the state and cleanliness of uniform the guest can judge a lot about hotel. it can be positive or negative judgement we can conclude that housekeeping department contributes greatly to all guest impression of the hotel.

Layout of the Housekeeping Department: Layout also aims to convey important areas co-ordinated by housekeeping departments.

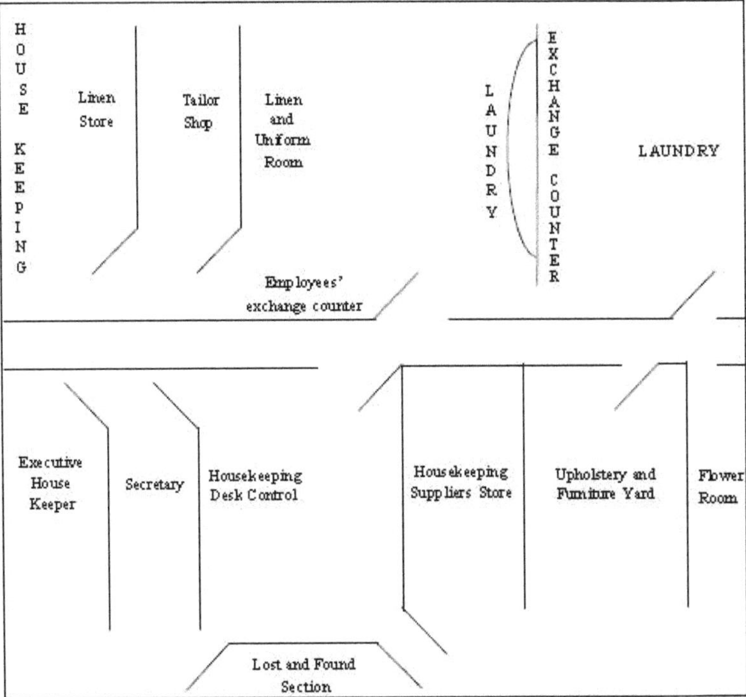

The layout given in Figure above indicates the functioning departments of housekeeping like linen store supported by tailor's shop; laundry supporting the exchange counter; housekeeping desk control equipped with as many telephone lines as possible so that messages pertaining to the housekeeping personnel may be noted and passed down to them without any delay. Housekeeping also controls lost and found section , wherein all items lost or found by the guests are reported and recorded properly.

To ensure smooth supply and functioning of housekeeping department its store shall be well equipped. Following items can be taken as a sample for this:

Night spreads	:	1 for every bed,
Sheets	:	2 for every bed,

Pillow case	:	2 for every bed,
Bath towel	:	1 for every guest,
Face towel	:	1 for every guest,
Hand towel	:	1 for every guest,
Bath mats	:	1 for every guest,
Mattress protectors	:	only a few to replace.

Upholstery and furniture yard is also an important section of housekeeping department with the prime duties to maintain and replace as and when furniture or any other replacement of furnishing is required in any room as is reported by room attendants. Another important part of this department is the flower room, equipped with a washing area and air conditioning to maintain freshness of flowers needed for decorative purpose.

As far as ideal number of personnel to be deployed in each section of housekeeping is concerned following formula can be used as a sample:

Executive Housekeeper	:	1 for 300 rooms
Assistant Executive Housekeeper	:	2 for 300 rooms
Floor Supervisor	:	1:30 Morning Shift 1:60 Night Shift
Public Area	:	1 for every shift
Linen/Uniform Room Supervisor	:	1 for every shift
Linen/Uniform Room Helper	:	1 for every shift
Room Attendant	:	1 for every fourteen rooms
Linen Attendant	:	1 for every shift
Housemen	:	1:60 rooms/per shift
Desk Attendant	:	1 for every shift
Tailor	:	subject to load
Horticulturist	:	One
Upholster	:	One
Head Gardner	:	1 for every 20
Gardner	:	1 for each 450 sq. ft. of landscape area

Q2. How do you manage guest amenities en-route and at the tourist destination?

Ans. All the hotels basically have a list of facilities that they provide to the guests in every room. It is the responsibility of the housekeeping department that they should provide all kinds of consumable as well as the assets kind of product in the rooms of the guest. In the given diagram we are giving the list of such of the items which are very essential in all kinds of operations in the hotel.

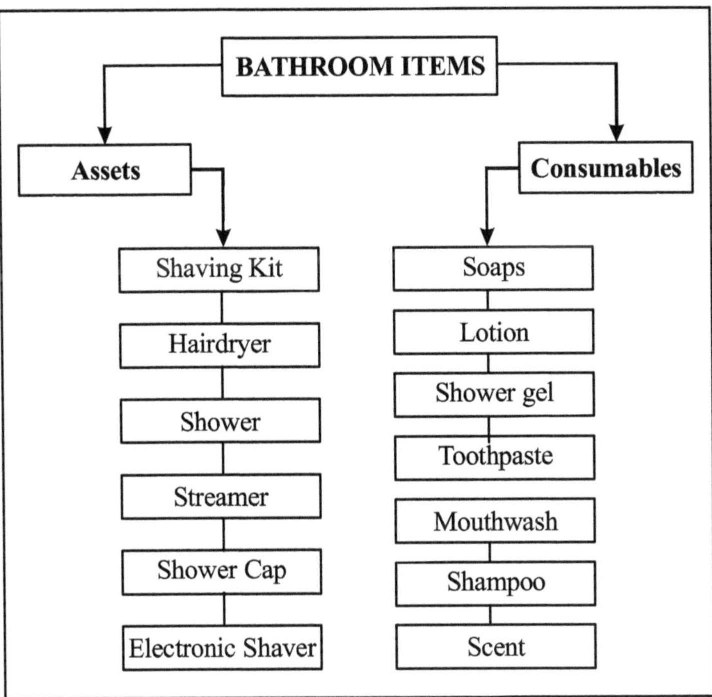

In the bedroom we should provide mainly assets to our customer by which the consumer can take the proper advantage in the room.

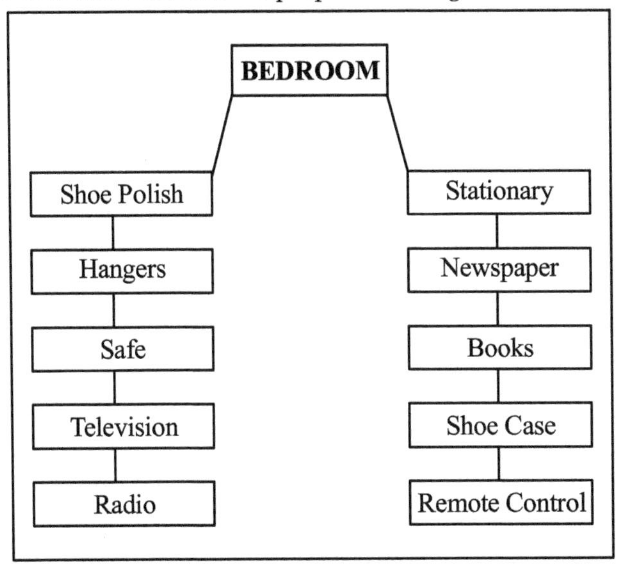

The food and the beverage mainly have the consumable kind of the product mainly but the equipments used in this area are mainly count as the assets.

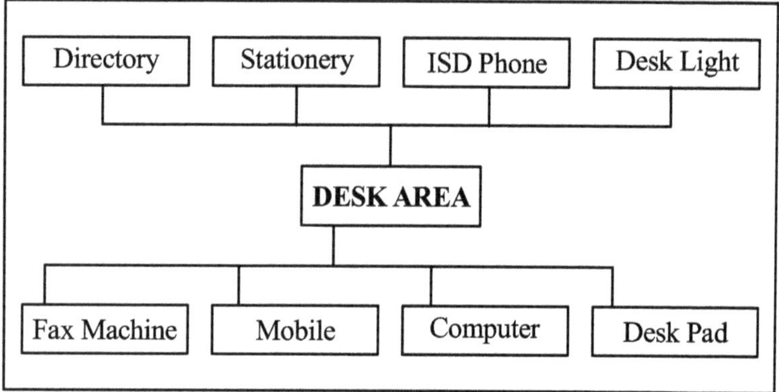

It is very important that we should provide the all kinds of amenities to each and every department in the organisation but only giving the amenities in not only the task of the housekeeping department. It is very much essential that they should manage all kind of things in the hotel. It is better for them that they should know that what is the requirement of which department.

Entry	Desk Top	Mini Bars	Cabinet	Near by Table	Setting Area	On Request
Don't disturb	Directory	Glasses	Laundry bags	ISD telephone	Television	Adaptors
Card	Fire escape plan	Bottle opener	Dry cleaning bags	Control panel's	Remote control	Heaters
Menu	Guidebook	Water	Shoe polish	Radio channels	Rack	Goggles
Fire escapeplan	Breakfast menu	Ice bucket	Shoe horn	Phone directory	Magazines	Swimsuit
Rules and	Ball pen	Napkins	Hanger's		Flowers	Racks
Regulations	Match box	Red wineglass	Shopping bags			Comb
	Folder and	Stirrers				Shaving cream
	Stationery					Razor
						iron

For the proper management of the function it is very much important that the management should make the proper checklist by which they can check all the things related with the hotel like these kind of checklist system.

Date..........	Room
Bath room checking	Recover' item
Bath towels.........	....
Hand towels.......	....
Face towels.........	....
Tumblers...........	....
Soap dish..........	....
Shoe shines kit.....	....
Slippers...........	....
Shaving socket....	....

Chapter-14

MANAGING FOOD AND BEVERAGE OPERATIONS

Q1. "Food and beverage operations are the same in the 5 star hotels and non-star hotels." Is the above statement correct or wrong? Answer with examples.

Ans. Food and beverage section of hospitality industry is mainly concerned with providing food and beverages to their consumers. Various elements related in its operations can be summarised in thecatering cycle which is shown in Figure.

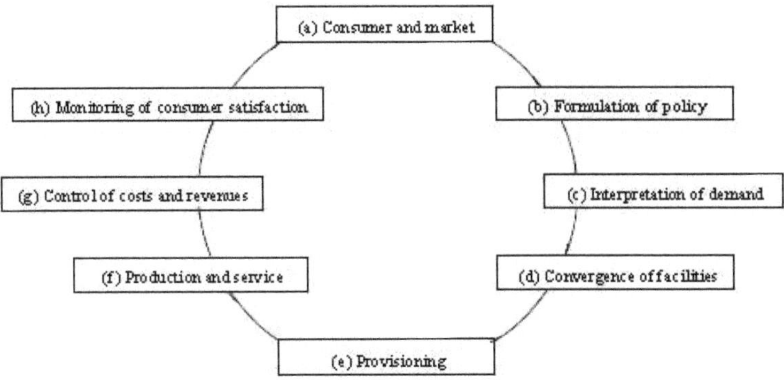

The fact that the catering cycle is not only concerned with operations but it is also a dynamic model in the sense that any one problem in one section of the cycle will cause difficulties for other elements of the cycle. For example, problem in the purchase section will also affect production and service, while improper utilisation of raw materials during production would also affect control system and so on.

We can infer from the cycle that an ideal food and drink service would be one which:

- provides food and drink on demand;
- has optimum utilisation of labour and skill, raw materials and equipments;

- has quick and simple methods of operational design; and
- has flexible system design allowing ease of adaptation.

To be able to establish and manage such an ideal food and beverage outlet one would require meticulous preparation, both at pre and post opening stages of the outlet. Yet the common assumption is that Food and Beverage outlet is the easiest way to earn a profit, since food always sells. It is also often assumed that if you eat well then you know how to run an eating joint. Well such thoughts are

far from the truth. Let us now discuss various elements involved in the opening and running of a restaurant successfully.

Managing food service operations: As a manager you need to concentrate on the management aspect of food services once your outlet is operational. Various aspects of managing food service operations involves:

(1) Food Purchasing: According to John Stefanelli the food service purchasing involves:

- developing specifications;
- preparing an approved suppliers list;
- determining the appropriate order size; and
- establishing appropriate receiving and storage procedures.
- Specifications is the first step, since it represents cost and quality control guidelines.

Developing appropriate specifications for each item purchased from an outside supplier helps in avoiding any future misunderstanding among the concerned people. Mostly the restaurant manager's develop an approved supplier's list. This ensures a consistency in quality and cost.

This also helps in controlling the buyer's activities. Usually, the manager can only add or delete a supplier's name to the list. Determining the order size is very difficult. A case of over-buy results in storage problem whereas under-buy is an option no manager wants to take. Over a period of time a somewhat accepted order size could be agreed upon.

Once needs are determined, the procedure for ordering and buying is set up. Invoices and receipts with signatures will help in checking any possible mischief or theft.

(2) Managing food production systems: Food production is the core of the food service industry. The three different types of menus which are mainly used according to the nature of outlet.

Although menu forms the core of food service industry, the ingredients form the magic part of the food produced. Herein, comes the usefulness of recipe standardisation. It is the most important tool available to control costs and ensure product consistency and quality. Consistence duplication of food item is achieved with an accurate record of ingredients, amounts and methods of combining ingredients and cooking.

Although standardisation of a recipe is important, it is often overlooked in food service industry.

As a manager, you shall ensure that standardisation of a recipe is achieved so as to control quantity and quality along with the costs involved in running an eating joint.

(3) Food Service Hygiene: Hygiene is very important for any eating joint. Reputation of a restaurant is made based on its menu and hygiene. Here the employees are in constant contact with food and preparation equipment. Major source of contamination of food arises from human contact from elements like skin, fingernails, hair, jewellery, mouth, nose and respiratory tract and eyes. Employees, therefore, should be trained to ensure that they maintain personal hygiene.

Next area of consideration is the equipment to be used. The cleaning area should be clean so as to ensure food service hygiene. The sink and work surfaces should be cleaned before and after every use. The equipments should be sanitised and sterilised after every cleaning. These sterilised equipments need to be stored in a clean area with protection from splash, dust and contact with food. Various sanitation methods like thermal and chemical sanitation methods among others

should be used.

The kitchen area and dining space should be pest free. Pests like, mice, cockroaches, etc. bring bad reputation to a place because they are carrier of many diseases. Hence, regular pest control methods must be undertaken so as to ensure hygenity of not only food but also of the surroundings.

Beverages: Beverage is a liquid which is specifically prepared for human consumption. In addition to filling a basic human need, beverages form part of the culture of human society.

The beverages use in the hotel industry as well as to serve the guest at any occasion or function. It is a part of the hotel industry. In some countries like it is very important that we should take permission from the government or the concerned authority. In Delhi the department like Delhi Tourism Development Corporation also have the right to give the permission for the alcohol shop. If you are the hotel, bar or inn owner that it is very much required for you that you should take permission for that. The hotel should have the proper menu to give the details of the drinks they are serving. It is very important that we should clearly define all the tings. Sometimes a wine can create a problem with foods. So, it is our responsibility that we should make them clear that both the things should not serve together.

There are different types of beverages but they are mainly classified based on their properties and ingredients.

Broadly there are two types of beverages:

(1) Alcoholic Beverages and

(2) Non-Alcoholic Beverages.

Non Alcoholic Beverages: A non-alcoholic beverage is a beverage that contains no alcohol. Non-alcoholic mixed drinks are often consumed by children, people whose religion restricts alcohol consumption, recovering alcoholics, and anyone wishing to enjoy flavourful drinks without alcohol.

- Juices
- Shakes
- Coffee
- Mineral water
- Cocktail without alcohol
- Mixed drinks
- Aerated drinks etc.

Alcoholic Beverages: Some examples are given below:

An alcoholic beverage is a drink that normally contains alcohol in different proportions based on its type. They are generally divided in following given categories:

Beverage	Source
Brandy	Fruit juices
Whisky	Cereal grains
Rum	Molasses/sugarcane
Wines (Port, Sherry)	Grapes and other fruits
Beer	Cereals

The wines are known for their area. We call them with their area name also. It is very much requiring that we should make list for that because that will help us to serve the drink in a proper way. The list contains all the wines from common to the very much special. We can make the list in a way:

- List of wines from all countries and some classical collection
- Traditional wines of French, German, and Italian
- Modern prestigious wine
- Wine from some particular countries

Requirements before offering alcoholic beverages:

- Age clarification of the customer
- Service present in some fixed hours only
- Required license or any kind of permit that allows it.

We can also classify the drinks on the basis of their drinking time like:

(1) After Meal Drink: These kinds of drinks mainly work as a digestive tonic for the person. These kinds of drinks mainly taken just after the food. In this category of drink we mainly use the malt whiskey and brandy.

(2) Banqueting Wine Lists: These kinds of wine list have the variety according to the pocket of the customer. In this category we have a special drink to very common drink also. The banqueting list contains the wine of popular brand.

(3) Rooms' Service List: In room services list the number of brand should be minimum and list taken as bar list.

Purchasing of Beverages: While purchasing, most important thing is to decide the correct order. It should not be in excess because it can affect your evaluation method of sales. It can create the problem in serving to the customers properly. If we have the large amount of storage that affect our sales also

For this we can use a formula

$M = w(t + l) + s$

Where M shows maximum stock, w shows average usage rate, t shows review period, l shows lead time and s shows safety stock.

Pricing of Beverages: Three basic methods mare given for the pricing of beverages which are as follows:

(1) Centred to Market: It should be known that the product we are offering to the customer is being purchased at what price from other provider and what is the maximum price that the customer can give for that.

(2) Cost in Addition to Pricing: By adding the cost price percentage to the drink cost, selling price is obtained.

(3) Return Rate: It should be determined to check the viability of the business.

Factors Considered in Beverage Controls: There are given some factors regarding to the beverage control.

(1) All the records related to supplies and delivers.

(2) Maintenance of the records related to received goods from the cellar.

(3) To draw alcoholic beverages items from the cellar, registration form should be properly filled.

(4) Proper record regarding sales and the profits.

(5) Full record of the transactions between the restaurants and the bars.

(6) Maintenance of stock record.

Factors Determining Good Cellar

Storage Management: Wine cellar is storage space where wines are stored. Many management.

(1) Cleaning of pipes and engines

(2) Drawing off the bear left in pipes

- Cleaning of the cellar equipments
- Even temperature range of about 13-15 centigrade
- Excess pressure on the cask should be reduced using spilling.
- Excellent Ventilation
- Cleaning of the beerlines after some fixed time etc.

Some storage examples

Type	Storage
Table wines	Tin contact with cork in bin
Rose wines	Coolest part of the cellar
Red wines	Upper bins
Spirits, beers, Juices etc.	upright in their containers.

Cost Control: Cost control refers to minimize the cost and increase the profit of any organisation. basically three types of costs included in a food service industry which are:

(1) Buying the raw material in an accurate quantity should be considered.

(2) Cost related to workers or labour is also there. Workers should be well trained in their work, it will reduce the cost but on the other hand they are not good then it will tend to loss of time material and extra cost due to damage occurred.

(3) Third is the menu cost. Which depends on the competition in the market, demand of customers. Simply if there is lack of competitors in the market then cost will be large due to monopoly but if there are many competitors for the same product then price would be low comparatively.

Q2. Food and Beverage operations are essential to hospitality business. Comment.

Ans. It takes care of the food and beverages that are procured or prepared by the hotel and served. Food and beverages manager, chefs, waiters all form a part of this department. The materials, tools technique and the labour are properly used. They are used to provide the food and drink on the demand of the consumers. The entire element in the food and beverage operations are related with each other without these operations we can't be able to do the things in a proper manner. So, it is very much required that we should adopt a kind of policies by which we can make all the things in a proper manner. It is very much required that all the operations of the food and the beverages should be done in a manner by which they can satisfy the customer in a proper manner. We should satisfy the need and wants of the customer when they wants. The food and the beverages departments should work in a manner by which they utislise their present resources in a proper manner. We should make a kind of system which is easy to adopt for all the people present in the system.

The operations are listed below:

(1) Positioning of the outlet in the hotel.

(2) Controlling the cost and revenues in the internal process.

(3) Consumer needs identifications'.

(4) Policies for profit making.

(5) Production and the service.

(6) Consumer satisfaction.

(7) Facilities.

(8) Proper identification of the demand.

❑❑❑

Chapter-15

MANAGING HOSPITALITY OPERATIONS: UNORGANISED SECTOR

Q1. Describe hospitality operations with suitable examples.

Ans. Hospitability industry today is a huge industry providing home facilities away from home to millions of travellers. These travellers can be segmented into various categories like business travellers, tourists, etc. All have different needs and expectations. However, the hospitality industry is so versatile that it is catering to the needs of all of them. The demand for inexpensive lodging has primarily given rise to the over increasing size of unorganised sector of hospitality industry. The number of unorganised hotels and rooms are three to four times than organised sector in Indian hospitality industry. Their prime types can be classified as:

- **Hotels owned by individuals:** According to the last census of 1990 conducted by the Department of Tourism, Government of India, there were approximately 11 lakhs such unorganised and unapproved units in India who were supplementing the handful of hotels registered in organised sector.
- **Guest Houses:** Government run guesthouses offer inexpensive accommodation and at times free accommodation to the government employees.
- **Youth Hostels:** These provide travellers with overnight lodgings at rock-bottom prices. Facilities are extremely basic guests have to provide their own bedding, share a communal washroom and prepare their own meals – yet youth hostels remain popular with students and other travellers with limited budgets.
- **Mansions:** are private homes that have been converted into guesthouses. They offer meals and lodging in an informal family atmosphere. Found primarily in Europe and Latin America, they are usually less expensive than hotels of comparable quality.
- **Bed and Breakfast:** accommodations are available throughout the British Isles and the idea has recently caught on in the United

States. Bed and breakfast guests can expect a full breakfast, a comfortable room and a shared bathroom.

- **Resort Condominiums:** a comparatively recent addition to the industry's product line, offer an alternative to hotel accommodations in Florida, Hawaii, Colorado and other popular vacation areas. Condominiums are individually owned residential units under common management within a multi-unit project. Owners often use them for vacations and rent them out the rest of the year.

  Condominiums provide apartment-style accommodations, with kitchen facilities, and recreational amenities either on-site or nearby.
- **Time Sharing:** The concept of time sharing was introduced first in Europe, then spread to the United States in the mid-1970s. It differs from the condominium concept in the sense that an individual does not own a complete unit but shares ownership with several other people. Each owner buys a vacation segment (usually two weeks) for a guaranteed number of years. Segments are scheduled so that only one owner uses the property at a time. Some time sharing companies allow clients to exchange segments with people.

The above classification of accommodation establishments is based on the range of facilities and the quality of services that these establishments offer to its customers. But many-a-times the facilities overlap and thus the classification becomes difficult. Nevertheless the broad classification remains the same.

These various establishments follow the same process of operating the departments, like, the F&B division, front office-cum-reception, housekeeping and maintenance. Only the strength of the employees varies. At times in a guesthouse, one cook would be preparing all types of food and front office is most of the times managed by the owner to give a personal touch. Thus, daily meetings can be held so as to provide solution to the problems being faced by the operational departments since the owner is constantly available in the establishment

Q2. How do you manage hospitality operations in the unorganized sector?

Ans. It is very essential for the hotel industry that they should use the appropriate information present in the market. Some time the wrong information can affect you. Most the data and information present in the market are misleading. For the information purpose we should train our people with all kinds of method.

Price Decisions: The small hotels should take the proper decision in terms of the price of the package they are selling to the customer. The price of their package and the service should give the competition to the beg hotels. They should maintain in a manner by which the customer get the high amount of service and value in terms of the price we are charging to them. You should give the offers as well as the value added service to your customer.

Build a guest loyalty in term of the price: when we talk about the hotel industry it is very essential for the hotel that they should develop a kind of guest loyalty in terms of the price they are charging with the customer. The hotel should make a guest appreciation programme. To develop the relationship with the customer we should give those gifts and the free value service time to time. For that we should know who our loyal guest is.

Way to increase the revenue: it is very important for us that we should know the method to increase the revenue of our hotel. When the demand of the rooms is low it is better to decrease the price but due price because it can affect you in the near future. To decide the price of your service and the product you should test and research in the market.

Raise yourself up to high rated market: it is very important for us that we should make our hotel up to that standard by which we can target our customer by providing them a quality of service and the product. It is very essential that we should make positioning of our brand in the mind of the customer.

Use of the internet: most of the small size hotels do not look toward the web or the internet site available in the market by which are lacks of competition from the big hotels present in the industry. It is very important for the small hotels that they should make themselves familiar with the new day concept of marketing because in these days most of the tourists use the internet before going for any king of trip or tour. If you are aware of the internet you can market your hotels by the help of the internet which also enables to give you the facility to make identity in the mind of the customer.

When the small hotels come into the market it is very tough to them to make an identity in the mind of the customer it is very important for them that they should adopt a kind of policy and the existence of change present in the market. Sometime due to new kind of policy and the existence of change the business of small hotels can be affected they are not having a large amount of budget for their infrastructure but by the help of good strategy and the concepts they can maximise the business of their hotels. In India the unorganized sector of hotels in very large but due to lack of information about the policy and the strategy they can't be able to make themselves able to deal with the high class tourist. It is responsibility of the government that they should provide the proper help to small scale hotels for their growth and the development. Without the help from the government side these hotels cannot grow with a very fast rate proper utilization of resources should be the main motto for these small hotels cannot grow with a very important that they should promote their service and the product by the help proper media and channel. So, by the help of proper strategy and policy these small hotels also are able to grow faster.

❑❑❑

QUESTION PAPERS

MTM-13: TOURISM OPERATIONS
June, 2020

Note : Attempt any five questions in about 600 words each. All questions carry equal marks.

Q1. Discuss the concept of quality management in tourism. As a manager, how will you implement quality management strategies in your organ

Q2. Write short notes on any two of the following:

(a) Benefits of tourism to local community

(b) Elements in tourism operations

(c) Departmentalisation of an agency

Q3. Discuss various procedures associated with inbound tour operations.

Q4. Discuss the planning and preparation involved in providing and managing escort services for a tour.

Q5. Explain the various sources of earning for a travel agency.

Q6. What do you understand by Electronic Front Office (EFO) ? Discuss the significance of computerization and consequent interdependence of the front office with other departments.

Q7. Discuss the functions of the housekeeping department of a large-sized hotel.

Q8. Write short notes on any two of the following:

(a) The catering cycle

(b) Cost control

(c) Computer Application in F & B services

Q9. Discuss the prime types of hospitality organizations in unorganized sector. Also mention the features of services rendered iri this sector.

Q10. What is the importance of promotional campaigns in tourism ? Discuss some major activities in travel agencies.

❑❑❑

MTM-13: TOURISM OPERATION
February, 2021

Note : Attempt any five questions in about 600 words each. All questions carry equal marks.

Q1. What do you understand by distribution system ? Explain the role of distribution channels in tour operations.

Q2. Discuss the various operations handled by a manager for running a travel agency.

Q3. Write a detailed note on outbound tour operations.

Q4. Discuss the relationship between travel agencies and tourist transport suppliers.

Q5. Write short notes on any two of the following:

(a) Marketing Communications

(b) Public Relations

(c) Organisation of a Hotel

Q6. Define Reservation System with the help of a diagram. Discuss its various types.

Q7. Explain the organisation structure of the Housekeeping Department of a large sized hotel with the help of a diagram. Also discuss the prime duties of the key players of Housekeeping Department.

Q8. Explain the various aspects of managing food service operations.

Q9. Write a detailed note on positioning and promotion in unorganised sector.

Q10. Discuss in brief, various activities involved in managing in-house operations of a tour operator.

❑❑❑

MTM-13: TOURISM OPERATIONS
December, 2021

Note : Answer any five questions in about 600 words each. All questions carry equal marks.

Q1. Describe the external factors that affect the tour-operation businesses. Give examples to substantiate your answer.

Q2. What do you understand by Quality Management ? What is the role and importance of quality management in tourism operations ? Give examples.

Q3. Discuss the importance of managing business correspondence and linkages with service suppliers in tourism operations. Explain with the help of examples.

Q4. As a tour escort, how would you plan and manage a tour ? Explain with the help of an example.

Q5. Write short notes on any two of the following in about 300 words each:

(a) Distribution System in Tourism

(b) Customer Care in Tourism

(c) Managing Vouchers

Q6. Discuss the use of technology in Travel Agency operations.

Q7. What do you understand by organised and unorganised sector in hospitality operations? How can hospitality operations in the unorganised sector be managed?

Q8. What do you understand by 'Reservation Systems' in the context of a hotel set-up? Describe the functions of a Reservation department of a hotel.

Q9. Describe the organisation and layout of Housekeeping Department.

Q10. Write short notes on any two of the following in about 300 words each:

(a) Menu Planning

(b) Guest Cycle

(c) Marketing Communications in Travel Agency

❑❑❑

MTM-13: TOURISM OPERATIONS
June, 2022

Note : (i) Answer any five questions. (ii) All questions carry equal marks.

Q1. Define Tour Operation. Illustrate the contribution of tour operators in Indian tourism industry.

Q2. Describe the organisational structure and main functions of a tour operator.

Q3. Discuss the various functions and operations associated with front office in a hotel.

Q4. Write notes on the following:

(a) Costing of FIT tour package

(b) E-ticketing

Q5. Describe the procedure for designing and developing an escorted tour package.

Q6. Define quality management. Elaborate its objectives and importance in tour operation business.

Q7. Write a note on Major Hotel Chains and MNCs in tourism.

Q8. Illustrate the procedure for setting up of a tour operation business in India.

Q9. Elaborate the use and importance of technology in tour operation.

Q10. Write notes on the following:

(a) CRS

(b) Guest cycle in tourism business

❑❑❑

www.ingramcontent.com/pod-product-compliance
Ingram Content Group UK Ltd.
Pitfield, Milton Keynes, MK11 3LW, UK
UKHW021658190726
13853UKWH00001B/333